D1573054

Ohio in Historic Postcards

Along the Ohio Canal.

Ohio in Historic Postcards

SELF-PORTRAIT OF A STATE

H. Roger Grant

The Kent State University Press

KENT, OHIO, & LONDON, ENGLAND

© 1997 by

The Kent State

University Press,

Kent, Ohio 44242

ALL RIGHTS RESERVED

Library of Congress Catalog

Card Number 96-27747

ISBN 0-87338-569-1

Printed in Canada

04 03 02 01 00 99 98 97   5 4 3 2 1

Library of Congress Cataloging-in-Publication Data

Grant, H. Roger, 1943–

  Ohio in historic postcards : self-portrait of a state / H. Roger Grant

  p.   cm.

  ISBN 0-87338-569-1 (alk. paper)

  1. Ohio—History—Pictorial works. 2. Postcards—Ohio.

I. Title.

F492.G73   1997

977.1'041'0222—dc20   96-27747

British Library Cataloging-in-Publication data are available.

To George W. Knepper

Contents

Preface

❧ ❧ ❧

The preparation of this album book has been a pleasant experience. A sizable number of these images of Ohio from the formative part of the twentieth century comes from the collection of Claibourne E. Griffin, retired dean of the Buchtel College of Arts and Sciences at The University of Akron and a longtime postcard enthusiast. Clay freely permitted me to select those items that I wished to use. The remaining cards are mine, acquired at antique shops, auctions, flea markets, and paper and postcard shows.

A former colleague at The University of Akron, George W. Knepper, who probably knows more about the history of Ohio than any other person, read the manuscript and made valuable suggestions. His keen insights were wonderful, and his assistance saved me from embarrassing errors.

This book is organized into two sections: an introduction and the album. The former contains essays on the picture postcard and Ohio during the early years of the century. The latter, the heart of the volume, consists of ten sections with a brief commentary preceding each unit. Although I made an effort to maximize the number of Ohio communities and to achieve balance among regions, I sought most of all to select cards that effectively reveal everyday life in the state.

Introduction

The Picture Postcard in Ohio

The purchase of picture or "souvenir" postcards at an amusement park, bookstore, or restaurant is hardly a new experience for Ohioans. For nearly a century people have been attracted to the inexpensive and convenient means of sending "greetings" from virtually anywhere. But the decade beginning about 1905 was the heyday of the postcard in America, a short-lived Golden Age, and during this time view cards became highly collectable and filled albums throughout the land.[1]

As with most consumer items, there were forerunners to what became the ubiquitous picture postcard. During the Civil War era there were efforts to create "correspondence cards," copying trends in Europe, and in 1873 the United States Post Office introduced the "penny postal." This piece of heavy paper of approximately three by five inches was cheaper to send than a letter and thus immediately caught the public's fancy. The federal government profited from the innovation and attempted to monopolize card sales.

Private parties, however, took advantage of penny postcards. They purchased from the Post Office uncut sheets of cards and printed their message on the reverse side. When Italian Americans in Akron in 1884 decided to throw a "Mid-Summer Night's Pleasure Party," they arranged to have an elaborate announcement printed on the back of government postals. Select members of the Akron Italian community received a handsome invitation card that described an outing on the *City of Akron*, a steam-powered launch that operated locally on the Ohio and Erie Canal and on Summit Lake.

The pleasing and practical invitation card was reminiscent of the widely distributed trade card, a legacy of the Centennial Exposition in Philadelphia in 1876. These pieces of heavy paper, usually smaller than the recently introduced postcard, typically sported on one side fancy artwork, often in color and designed to capture public attention, and on the reverse information about the product, service, or firm. Because of their attractiveness, trade cards were commonly saved or passed along to others. Reaching their zenith of popularity during the 1880s, trade cards had largely disappeared from circulation by the end of the nineteenth century. The availability of other more cost-effective methods of reaching consumers caused the trading cards' demise. Growth of mass-produced newspapers and magazines gave advertisers better means of spreading their messages. Still, some publicists liked the concept of the trade card and adopted the picture-type postcards as advertising tools.

While trade cards were giveaways, the public had to purchase picture postcards. The first opportunity to buy cards, usually for a nickel, came at the World's Columbian Exposition in Chicago in 1893, an event that took the nation by storm.

Using a product that was already widely available in Europe, especially in Germany, where printing technologies were highly developed and postal regulations hospitable, the "pioneer cards" of the gala Chicago fair portrayed the range of attractions, including the much ballyhooed Ferris wheel.[2]

While picture postcards gained immediate popularity as inexpensive souvenirs, there were some drawbacks. Immediately apparent was that these pictorials used the inferior paper stock of the government cards. Moreover, if any writing other than the address appeared, the Post Office demanded two cents for delivery, double what it charged for handling regular cards. Printers usually warned the public: "If Other Side [the reverse from the "address only" side] Contains Writing Use 2-cent Stamp, Otherwise 1-cent." Senders thus paid the full first-class letter rate. Furthermore, purchasers did not care to be charged postage for cards that they planned to keep.

The growing consumerism of the mid-1890s, which shortly blossomed into the massive and durable progressive movement, helped change restrictive postal policies. In May 1898 Congress passed the Private Mailing Card Act, which granted makers of privately printed postcards the same rate as the government issues. A view card could now be sent for a penny. "The 1898 date is a natural division point for American cards," concluded a student of pioneer view cards, "making the start of easier days and wider use after years of battling unjust rates and regulations which made every publishing effort a financial gamble and completely discouraged most of those who tried it."[3]

Another federal boost to what unquestionably had developed into a national mania came a decade after the rate adjustment. This involved how the picture postcard could be used. Heretofore the Post Office prohibited senders from writing on the *reverse* side, with the admonition "This Side for the Address" written in that space. But in 1907 the Post Office permitted the "split" or "divided" back. No longer did senders need to pen a few sentences on the front, often despoiling the pictorial image; now they could have half of the back for their messages. The cards came with two clearly defined parts: "This Space May Be Used for Communication" and "the Address Only to Be Written Here." The format of the modern picture postcard had fully evolved.[4]

It is difficult to explain why fads come and go. Fancywork and homemade crafts in the 1890s, dance halls and touring tent or circuit Chautauquas in the 1910s, crossword puzzles and Mahjong in the 1920s, and miniature golf and monopoly games in the 1930s found enthusiasts in Ohio as elsewhere. And while some of these manias remain firmly entrenched in popular culture, others followed a somewhat predictable course: the initial excitement, a peak in popularity, and the eventual decline.

Americans caught the bug of "postal carditis" early in the twentieth century and were afflicted by this collecting frenzy until about the time of the First World War. The years 1908 to 1912 likely marked the period of greatest excitement. While after this time picture postcards continued to be purchased, sent, and saved, the intensity, especially for collecting, waned.[5]

Several factors explain the popularity of picture postcards. Most everyone agreed that they were physically attractive. Cards printed in color provided a pleasant change from typical images, whether stereopticon slides, commercial portraitures, or newspaper and magazine illustrations. A majority of color cards sold domestically came from Germany, where they were produced by specialists who excelled in color work. Printers in Bavaria and Saxony employed a process called chromolithography that permitted them to use vivid colors to create fine, detailed pictures.[6]

Card entrepreneurs also provided appealing black-and-white, sepia ("monochrome"), and tinted picture postcards. While they might be printed in the United States by such leading firms as Detroit Publishing and Rotograph, the cards frequently came from German concerns because of their superior quality and their competitive prices.[7]

Consumers purchased a wide range of picture postcards, finding pleasing ones to keep for themselves or to send to family members or friends. If cards were mailed, recipients usually were loath to throw away these eye-catching items. This practice of collecting explains the phenomenon of the souvenir postcard album, which by 1910 had become a prominent feature of most middle-class households, second in importance only to the family Bible. There were even "postal card sofa pillows" and wooden postals that were "scooped out in order to give receptacles in which may be concealed strips of photographs and pictures."[8]

The popular press abroad and in the United States commented on the positive aspects of the picture postcard craze. The English *Macmillan's Magazine* saw the view card as stimulating the masses, claimed that collecting was good: "We should not too readily condemn any fashion which acts in the direction of broadening interests and awaking enthusiasm for what may appear to some of us to be trifles but to them are the occasions of delight and of forgetfulness of irksome drudgeries." *The Ladies' Home Journal* encouraged its readers to donate their extra or unwanted cards to international church groups because of "the eagerness of foreign missionaries to receive bright-colored cards. There are places where a picture has never been seen, and great is the joy where even one is owned, though it be but a post card." In a lighter fashion, Rosalie Dawson noted in the *Woman's Home Companion* that picture postcards made entertaining parlor games.

> For the first game of the evening the hostess provided twelve picture postals, each of which was [of] . . . some subject of interest in some city of the United States. Only one object was selected from a single city. Thus Philadelphia gave the state house; New York, Grant's tomb; Boston, Harvard College, and so on. Each card was numbered. The players received pencils and paper. They were asked to write down the name of each celebrated object as they believed it to be, identifying it with the number of the card. The player answering the most names correctly won a pretty postal card case in brown linen, having the word "Postals" worked upon it in colored silks.[9]

Corresponding to the pleasing and intriguing properties of picture postcards was the rich variety of subjects and a multitude of views that became readily available. Prominent tourist attractions and scenes of larger cities enjoyed great popularity, and occasionally even high-quality views of a medium-sized community might be offered. About 1910 the hometown of martyred President William McKinley was the place to buy "Six Beautifully Colored Post Cards of Canton, Ohio—Perforated for Detaching." These images, printed in Germany, included the "McKinley Residence, Public Square, Court House, McKinley Monument, The Auditorium [and] The Post-Office." There were also mass-produced cards that showed animals, children, entertainers, military leaders, politicians, and "pretty girls" (some undeniably pornographic). Then there were seasonal and holiday cards, including those for Valentine's Day, Easter, Fourth of July, Thanksgiving, and Christmas. There were birthday cards, comic and novelty cards, and the enduring advertising cards. "When everything worth seeing had been photographed," explained a social commentator in 1906, "the makers put on the market . . . actresses, paintings, illustrated poems—in fact almost everything."[10]

Picture postcards of a more localized nature also appeared on the market, including views of accidents, fairs, floods, fires, and visits by celebrities. Those cards, however, usually were issued in a black-and-white format. Hometown photographers captured scenes and events that were then converted into postcards. Specifically, proprietors of card shops, drug stores, novelty emporiums, stationery shops, and other outlets sent photographs or negatives to firms nationally and internationally to be printed as postcards. Their subjects were nearly always ones that large purveyors of cards could not hope to, or did not want to, offer.

The ultimate freedom of choice in subject matter came with the real-photographic, or "real-photo," card. In 1902 the Eastman Kodak Company of Rochester, New York, introduced a heavy, photographic, postcard-size developing paper (3¼ by 5½ inches) that permitted the making of a crisp black-and-white image. Now negatives could be cheaply and easily printed onto photographic stock with postcard backs.[11]

The creation of individualized pictorial postals became even more convenient the next year when Kodak offered the first inexpensive postcard camera. Amateur photographers could use a "Folding Pocket No. 3A" to snap the intended subject. The next step, if desired, involved opening a small door and inscribing with a stylus a brief caption on the exposed postcard-size film. The final act in this quickly mastered process required making a contact print on postcard mailing stock. Kodak gladly provided this service for ten cents a card, and it soon faced competition.[12]

The price of the picture postal was an added attraction. While it was costly to purchase a special camera, film, and processing, commercial cards became so cheap that virtually everyone could afford them. The retail price ranged from a nickel to two for a nickel to even less. A stockpiling of European-printed cards in 1909, prompted by fears of tariff legislation by Congress, created a large surplus and forced importers, jobbers, and retailers to slash prices. A customer might pay as little as a nickel for ten cards. Some picture postals, though, cost nothing. These free cards were likely used for advertising or promotional purposes, merchants providing them at their places of business or mailing them to prospective customers. For example, in 1905 the *Cleveland Plain Dealer* offered sixteen different views of Cleveland at "No charge"; however, "A Post Card Coupon cut from The Plain Dealer gets you one card; 15 Coupons gets you the entire series."[13]

An appealing feature of the postcards, and any other piece of first-class mail, involved speed of delivery. Within Ohio this usually meant next-day or even same-day delivery. By the early years of the twentieth century, homes in larger communities enjoyed twice-daily (except weekend) service, and the commercial cores of major cities received delivery three times daily during the work week. Moreover, Rural Free Delivery (RFD), introduced in 1896, expanded rapidly after 1900, giving rural Americans access to direct mail service. In 1897 there were only forty-four RFD routes nationally, but six years later the number reached 12,507, and more routes followed. *The Independent,* a reform-oriented magazine, observed in 1903 that "No enterprise [RFD] ever undertaken in any country has been so free from taint of corruption." Inhabitants of smaller communities without letter carriers relied on the village postmaster to "put up" mail soon after it arrived from the depot and to bring an important piece of mail to a recipient's attention. Whether metropolis or hamlet, mail collections were regular. People knew that a pick-up would occur at 7:00 A.M., noon, 5:00 P.M., or other times and could plan accordingly.[14]

The vast network of railways that laced Ohio (9,581 miles of steam lines by 1908) facilitated rapid mail delivery. The Post Office Department, committed to excellence, made the Railway Post Office (RPO) car an effective tool in the delivery chain. These specially designed pieces of rolling stock allowed skilled and dedicated employees to sort postal cards, letters, and the like en route between terminals. An RPO car was part of the standard consist of passenger trains. On the great rail "speedways"—for example, between Pittsburgh and Chicago—solid "fast mails," consisting of both RPO and mail storage equipment, raced to their destinations. The peak of this rail-mail service nationally came in 1915, when twenty thousand clerks worked on approximately four thousand RPO cars that traveled over more than 215,000 miles of track. Electric interurbans, more common in Ohio than in any other state, sometimes carried mail, as did a few city trolley lines. When the train stood in the station, the public could even post a card or letter directly into the RPO car through a special slot marked "Mail."[15]

If the postcard traveled by rail, results were frequently impressive. Since some local post offices early in the century stamped the time and date when they received cards, the length of transit can be determined. For instance, one picture postcard left the Ashtabula post office at 8:30 A.M. on October 5, 1908, and arrived at 5:00 P.M. the same day in the post office at Clarksfield in Huron County. The journey was not direct, however. Lake Shore & Michigan Southern Railroad (New York Central System) passenger train No. 23, which left the Ashtabula station at 9:21 A.M., presumably carried the card to Monroeville, 114 miles from Ashtabula, reaching that destination at 12:36 P.M. The depot agent, or a postal employee, "worked" the mail and transferred the sack with the Clarksfield-bound card to passenger train No. 6 of the Wheeling & Lake Erie Railway. This train left Monroeville at 3:28 P.M., arriving in Clarksfield, fifteen miles away, at 4:02 P.M. Even if the trains were late, enough leeway time existed between the scheduled connections, and additional trains also served both rail lines.

The efficient mail delivery system permitted postcards to serve as reliable and convenient means of communication. The available alternatives possessed limitations. Take the telephone. Ownership in Ohio was not widespread in some areas until after the First World War. Problems arose in cities that had more than one telephone company, thus necessitating multiple hook-ups. And at this time long-distance telephone service was neither complete nor wholly dependable. Of course, an older option was the commercial telegraph. Like long-distance telephone calls, telegraphic messages were considered expensive. Moreover, custom restricted the sending of telegrams to emergencies or special events—health crises, deaths, births.

Postcards, then, offered people a convenient, practical, and inexpensive means of communicating everything from "I'll see you at Church on Sunday and can stay for dinner" to "You have a cordial invitation to a party at my home Sat. Eve. Be sure and come if you can" to "Will not be there for the picnic. Would like to but can't." If mailed from a town within a hundred miles or so, these cards surely would be received the next day, or even the same day, giving the recipient ample time to respond.

There were only a few problems with the postcard format, whether pictorial or plain. During the height of postals' popularity, some people believed that Post Office employees read the messages, and this concern explains why a few were written in a foreign language or code. Occasionally someone, like George Fitch in

1906 on the pages of *American Magazine,* lamented that the postals threatened the art of letter writing, which was never well-developed in America: "Like a heaven-sent relief, the souvenir postal card has come to the man of few ideas and a torpid vocabulary. But now arises a new danger which threatens even this last citadel of letter writing [the love letter]. The souvenir postal card courtship, if not an accomplished fact, is only a step in the future. Already a conversation a year long can be maintained at a cost of one cent per day in postage and from three to five cents in cards."[16]

Americans' enthusiasm for picture postcards, however, especially as collectibles, slipped noticeably by the First World War. Like other fads, the novelty had run its course. Also, after about 1913, the pictorial postal faced competition from the newly introduced greeting card, which offered complete privacy. And then there was the war. The conflict disrupted commerce between Germany and the United States making German-manufactured cards virtually unobtainable. Moreover, when America entered the fighting in April 1917, the national mood took on a somber tone. The purchase of "gay" or "sweet" cards ranked low on lists of personal priorities.[17]

American producers filled an ever-smaller void with inferior cards. Admittedly, some domestic concerns had provided competitive products, but they lacked the overall excellence of German ones. For example, American postals frequently came with unattractive white borders, a move inspired by the desire to save ink.

Quality continued to erode. "Linen" cards of the 1930s and 1940s possessed little aesthetic appeal. A card historian described them as "probably the ugliest and most grotesque ever made. . . . The linen effect of the surface made all clarity of detail impossible. The colors were artificial and never attractive." Then came "chrome" views, with their smooth, glossy finish, which, according to one collector, "have about as much charm as a marble floor." Nothing replicated the finest cards of Germany. Also gone were the real-photo views. Camera enthusiasts moved on to new photographic equipment, and by the early 1940s film for postcard-making had generally become unavailable.[18]

Eventually there was a resurgence of interest in the picture postcard. During the 1960s the allure of these historic artifacts created a major revival in card collecting. But the fascination was for cards from "the Golden Age," not for contemporary ones. This renewed passion led to discoveries of cards long laid away in attics and bureau drawers and to the launching of postcard collecting clubs, "shows," and publications. Prices soared, and some enthusiasts considered historic cards to be a sound financial investment.

Ohio in the New Century

In the early twentieth century many Ohioans were optimistic about the future of their state. The years of awful economic conditions that had followed the Wall Street panic of May 1893 were largely unpleasant, distant memories; the upturn in business about the time of that "splendid little war" with Spain in 1898 seemed to be the harbinger of comfortable years to come. While a modest economic downswing occurred in 1903 and was followed four years later by a more severe, albeit brief, "banker's panic," these events caused only limited interruptions to the unrivaled prosperity Ohioans commonly experienced during the first two decades of the century.

Anyone who wished to tout Ohio's virtues between the Spanish-American War and the First World War had ample evidence from which to chose. The most obvious was population: the state claimed 4,157,545 residents in 1900, which made it the fourth most inhabited state, after New York, Pennsylvania, and Illinois. That same federal census revealed that Ohio ranked fifth in manufacturing, with 345,869 people employed in creating products worth approximately $830 million (the national total was about $11 billion). Ohio workers produced a vast array and quantity of products, including agricultural implements, bicycles, boots and shoes, cigars, glass, iron and steel, machine screws, matches, mattresses, pumps, sewing machines, sewer pipes, steam shovels, tires, wagons, and watches. Additionally, residents exploited the state's natural resources, especially clay, limestone, sandstone, salt, and oil and gas. But most of all they relied on coal. By 1910 the annual production of these "black diamonds," the basic fuel for industry and transportation, totaled 30,544,346 long-tons (2,240 pounds); only Pennsylvania, West Virginia, and Illinois produced more coal.[19]

While mineral production was usually regionalized, the location of manufacturing endeavors knew no geographical bounds. Ohio had numerous industrial communities. Cleveland and Cincinnati, with populations in 1900 of 381,768 and 325,902, respectively, were nationally recognized centers of manufacturing. Akron, Canton, Columbus, Dayton, Lima, Toledo, Youngstown, and Zanesville were among other ever-expanding loci of production.[20]

Early in the century numerous Ohio metropolises seemed destined for real greatness. "Go-getters" and "live-wires" inhabited these places, and their civic pride, hard work, and business acumen augured well for the future growth and prosperity of their hometowns. Marion, in the north-central section, with a population of 11,862 in 1900, and internationally famous for production of steam shovels, typified these dynamic communities. The future president of the United States, Warren G. Harding, publisher of the *Marion Star,* tirelessly labored to boost the

Marion County capital, and the pages of his daily newspaper regularly extolled the promise of the place. "[Marion is] an aggressive, hustling and striking example of the thoroughly wide awake American city," concluded a promotional writer for the Columbus, Delaware & Marion Electric Railroad in 1908. "[Marion] maintains more miles of paved streets than any other place of its size in the country and its manufactured products are exported to all parts of the world. It has practically doubled its population in the last ten years and the business men of the community are keenly awake to the commercial possibilities of this enterprising center of mercantile activity."[21]

Boards of trade, businessmen's associations, and chambers of commerce flourished throughout the state, their purpose being to attract and keep industries and to improve the overall quality of life in Ohio's towns. In 1911, for example, the Newark Board of Trade sponsored the Licking County seat's first Arbor Day and Clean Up Day. The group also raised money for the court house park improvement and the library endowment and promoted the "Good Roads Movement," a local hospital, and the Young Woman's Christian Association.[22]

The state's industrial communities were conveniently linked to sources of raw materials and leading marketplaces, particularly those on the East Coast and in the Midwest. "As a manufacturing state Ohio has many advantages," observed Oscar Straus, the United States Secretary of Commerce and Labor in 1907. "The lakes on the north, the Ohio river on the south, and the canals furnish an abundant means of water transportation, and the railroad facilities are unsurpassed. Coal and iron, those two important factors in manufactures, are easily obtainable. Moreover, the location of the state with regard to a market for its products is excellent."[23]

Businesses in Ohio enjoyed more than a splendid geographical position, however; they profited from access to a growing and diverse work force. Thousands of country boys left their family farms for jobs typically in the big and medium-sized industrial cities. These positions were usually their first wage-earning experiences. The Van Sweringen brothers, Oris Paxton Van Sweringen (1879–1936) and Mantis James Van Sweringen (1881–1935), for example, who hailed from rural Wayne County, made their fortunes in Cleveland as real estate developers and railroad executives. Masses of semi- and unskilled immigrants, often from central, eastern, and southern Europe, flocked to urban Ohio and readily found employment in a plethora of concerns. By the outbreak of the Great War, it was common to find Hungarians toiling in foundries, Slovenes in steel mills, and Italians in railway shops. Cleveland, most of all, became a truly "ethnic" metropolis with approximately three-quarters of its residents being first- and second-generation non-native-born Americans. "Cleveland isn't a city," argued one wag. "It's a collection of ethnic villages."[24]

But not everyone in Ohio lived in cities. While the size of the state's rural population continued to diminish, in 1900 about a third of Ohioans still were on farms. The large agricultural sector gave the state a balanced economic base, making Ohio both urban and rural, factory and farm.[25]

Since frontier times agriculture had sustained the Ohio economy. The transportation revolution that began prior to the Civil War prompted agrarians to produce more products for commercial markets, abandoning the largely subsistence work that commonly characterized the pioneer years of farm life. And the market-oriented process accelerated. By the early twentieth century, Buckeye State farmers were fully accustomed to a market economy and took advantage of a splendid transportation network, one considerably enhanced by the appearance of the electric "interurban." These intercity trolleys, with their frequent and dependable service, especially helped producers of dairy products, poultry, and other perishable or seasonal commodities.

Resembling other states in the Midwest, Ohio farmers were not tied to a single crop; thus, they did not suffer from the evils attendant to a one-crop economy. Ohioans responded to the food needs of an expanding urban population, becoming heavily involved in dairying and corn-hog production. The number of milk cows rose from 654,000 in 1870 to approximately 800,000 in 1910; the output of corn increased from 67,501,000 bushels in 1869 to 157,513,000 bushels in 1909; and the swine population grew from 1,729,000 in 1870 to 3,106,000 in 1910.[26]

Ohio agrarians benefited not only from diversification but also from the "parity years" of 1909–14, when American farmers were relatively free from those worries that had beset the preceding generation. When prosperity reigned, farmers acted optimistically. They named their farmsteads "Happy Valley Farm" or "Pleasant View Farm" or "Sunnydale." One country newspaper editorialized, "Farmers should stop and consider that it is a fine advertisement for any county to have a farm named. It gives tone to the surroundings and is evidence that the farmer takes pride in his home and is willing to vouch for the productive worth of his farm and surrounding territory."[27]

Life in rural Ohio could be good. In the late teens the farm publication *Country Gentleman* described conditions experienced by a Montgomery County dairyman and his family who lived about a dozen miles from Dayton. In addition to running water in the house and barn, a washing machine, and an interurban stop at the corner of the farm, this particular agrarian could brag about even more conveniences: "We have a rural [mail] route and a trunk-line telephone. A gasoline and oil tank goes by once a week. A bread wagon and a fish vendor from town comes several times a week. We have an electric light plant [operated by a gasoline engine]. A common school is within a five-cent [interurban] fare limit. Why should we want to live in a city? Our farm is ideal."[28]

But not everyone found Ohio to be a utopia in the waxing twentieth century. The state had its share of poor residents who lived in substandard housing, breathed impure air, and drank contaminated water. Conditions in sections of Cleveland, for example, were dreadful. "The city's health is in jeopardy as long as we have 234.5 miles of streets which have no sewers and 365.5 [miles] without pavement," reported a public health officer in 1902. "Dirty streets cannot be cleaned. The dust which rises from them is laden with germs. In time of an epidemic they become an actual danger. . . . Cleveland is a manufacturing center. The smoke that annoys us has made the city what it is, the metropolis of Ohio. Nevertheless this smoke is injurious to the lungs. But by far more injurious is the dust that flies through the air. The thorough cleaning of streets is a sanitary necessity."[29]

Bad physical environments contributed to troubling social conditions. Crime and vice festered. In 1905 a *Cleveland Plain Dealer* reporter believed that he had found the Ohio "hell-hole"—Canton: "Every outlawed amusement offered by Cincinnati is duplicated in Canton, and the smaller city has added a few frills. One section of a narrow street, not a block long, appropriately known as Whiskey alley, is lined with gambling dens, each located above a saloon. . . . Chicago boasts that Custom House place is the most wicked thing this side of Paris. A certain theater of Canton has all the characteristics of Custom House place. Cincinnati has nothing to equal it; Cleveland never had."[30]

While conditions in Canton and elsewhere had long spurred on vice crusaders and other moralists, increasing social problems, revealed in the growing gap between rich and poor in urban areas, sparked a significant social progressive crusade.

Washington Gladden, minister of the First Congregational Church in Columbus, did much to popularize the social gospel movement, a concept based on the teachings of Jesus Christ. These uplifters asked, "What would Jesus do?" The answer, of course, was that He would help those who suffered as best He could. Fuel yards, employment bureaus, and settlement houses appeared statewide, helping thousands to improve their lot.

A legacy of the five troubled years of the 1890s was a consumer's revolt that developed into a principal component of the progressive movement, that widespread housecleaning initiative that lasted from the late 1890s through the First World War. Ohioans, particularly city dwellers, resented large corporations', especially utilities, tax-dodging, poor service, and overall arrogance. Soon the shrill demands for reform—including ad valorem taxation, rate regulation, and even municipal ownership of quasi-public corporations—could be heard throughout the state. Understandably, Ohio voters backed scores of consumer-sensitive politicians, the most famous being Toledo mayor Samuel "Golden Rule" Jones (1897–1904) and Cleveland mayor Tom L. Johnson (1901–9). And Socialists, who represented "advanced progressivism," showed political strength and even captured power in a variety of communities, an example being their 1911 victory in the Auglaize County town of St. Marys.[31]

In 1912 the reform crusade reached the state level in a dramatic fashion. Delegates to a special constitutional convention held in Columbus drafted forty-one reform amendments and submitted them to the voters. Although not all of these proposals won approval, the altered constitution made Ohio a much more progressive place. The first gubernatorial administration of James M. Cox (1913–15) implemented the popular will of 1912. Residents received measures for home rule, direct democracy, and tax revisions. Ohio may not have been a banner progressive state like Iowa, Oregon, and Wisconsin, but it unmistakably demonstrated the prevailing spirit of reform.[32]

Ohio matured during the two decades that preceded the First World War, prospering and gaining enormous importance in the nation. Citizens predictably took pride in their native or adopted state. The approximately two hundred picture postcards, many of the real-photo variety, which compose the core album portion, offer a wide-ranging glimpse of how the landscape and the people of the Buckeye State appeared nearly a century ago. Although most commercial cards convey the attractive, even outstanding, features of Ohio, a few of local sponsorship or by amateurs capture less pleasant qualities. While the seamier side of daily life is usually absent from pictorial postals, the rich texture of the state is readily apparent. Fortunately, for anyone interested in the state's past, the Golden Age of picture postcards coincided with the making of modern Ohio.

Notes

1. The best general study of picture postcards is George Miller and Dorothy Miller, *Picture Postcards in the United States, 1893–1918* (New York: Clarkson N. Potter, 1976). See also Lyell D. Henry, Jr., *Was This Heaven?* (Iowa City: University of Iowa Press, 1995), 1–2.

2. J. R. Burdick, ed., *Pioneer Post Cards: The Story of Mailing Cards to 1898 with an Illustrated Checklist of Publishers and Titles* (Privately printed, 1957), 6–11, 14; Richard Carline, *Pictures in the Post* (Philadelphia: Deltiologists of America, 1972), 37–55.

3. Burdick, *Pioneer Post Cards*, 15.

4. Ray D. Applegate, *Trolleys and Streetcars on American Picture Postcards* (New York: Dover, 1979), v.

5. John Walker Harrington, "Postal Carditis and Some Allied Manias," *American Illustrated*

Magazine 61 (March 1906): 562–67; telephone interview with George N. Johnson, Jr., Buena Vista, Virginia, November 21, 1993.

6. Frank Staff, *The Picture Postcard & Its Origins* (New York: Praeger, 1966), 64–81.

7. Miller and Miller, *Picture Postcards in the United States,* 145–64.

8. Sander Davidson, "Wish You Were Here," *American Heritage* 13 (October 1962): 97–112; Harrington, "Postal Carditis and Some Allied Manias," 564.

9. "The Picture Post-Card," *Living Age* 242 (July 30, 1904): 311; Samuel D. Price, "What to Do with Your Post Cards," *The Ladies' Home Journal* 30 (March 1913): 98; Rosalie Dawson, "Fun with Picture Postal Cards," *Woman's Home Companion* 33 (February 1906): 56.

10. Harrington, "Postal Carditis and Some Allied Manias," 563.

11. Hal Morgan and Andreas Brown, *Prairie Fires and Paper Moons: The American Photographic Postcards, 1900–1920* (Boston: David R. Godine, 1981), xiii–xiv.

12. Johnson interview; *Chicago Tribune,* January 2, 1994.

13. Miller and Miller, *Picture Postcards in the United States,* 31.

14. "Advantages of Rural Free Delivery," *The Independent* 55 (March 5, 1903): 578–80.

15. Bryant Alden Long and William Jefferson Dennis, *Mail by Rail: The Story of the Postal Transportation Service* (New York: Simmons-Boardman, 1951), 1–80.

16. Johnson interview; George Fitch, "Upon the Threatened Extinction of the Art of Letter Writing," *American Magazine* 70 (June 1910): 174.

17. Miller and Miller, *Picture Postcards in the United States,* 26, 32.

18. Applegate, *Trolleys and Streetcars on American Picture Postcards,* vii; Johnson interview.

19. *Twelfth Census of the United States Taken in the Year 1900: Population,* Part 1 (Washington, D.C.: U.S. Census Office, 1901), 34; *Manufactures, 1905,* Part 2: *States and Territories* (Washington, D.C.: Government Printing Office, 1907), 827–83; *Ohio: An Empire Within an Empire* (Columbus: Ohio Development and Publicity Commission, 1950), 3; *Statistical Abstract of the United States 1915* (Washington, D.C.: Government Printing Office, 1916), 216, 829.

20. *Twelfth Census of the United States, 1900,* 308–10.

21. *Description and Photo Flashes of the Columbus, Delaware & Marion Electric Railroad* (Columbus: The Bloomer Bureau, n.d.), 75.

22. G. Wallace Chessman, "Town Promotion in the Progressive Era: The Case of Newark, Ohio," *Ohio History* 87 (Summer 1978): 269.

23. *Manufactures, 1905,* 827.

24. George W. Knepper, *Ohio and Its People* (Kent, Ohio: Kent State University Press, 1989), 286–312; David D. Van Tassel and John H. Grabowski, eds., *The Encyclopedia of Cleveland History* (Bloomington: Indiana University Press, 1987), xxix–xxxiii.

25. *Twelfth Census of the United States, 1900,* lxxxii, 305–21.

26. Robert Leslie Jones, "Ohio Agriculture in History," *Ohio History* 65 (July 1956): 244–45.

27. *Leetonia (Ohio) Reporter,* June 17, 1904.

28. *The Country Gentleman* 80 (January 5, 1918): 4.

29. *Annual Report of the Health Office Cleveland 1902,* 937–42.

30. *Cleveland Plain Dealer,* September 12, 1905.

31. Hoyt Landon Warner, *Progressivism in Ohio, 1897–1917* (Columbus: Ohio State University Press, 1964), 22–118; Nick Salvatore, *Eugene V. Debs: Citizen and Socialist* (Urbana: University of Illinois Press, 1982), 238–40, 264.

32. Knepper, *Ohio and Its People,* 333–35.

In July 1884 members of the Italian community of Akron received this private mailing postal. *(Ron Schieber)*

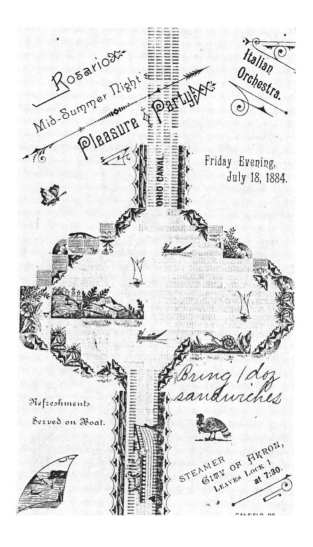

PUBLIC SQUARE

A purchaser of this picture postcard of Public Square in Cleveland is duly warned to use the back side for "address only;" however, the maker left space on the front for a brief message. *(H. Roger Grant)*

PLACE A
ONE CENT
STAMP
HERE

AUTHORIZED·BY·ACT·OF·CONGRESS·OF·MAY·19·1898

"POSTAL CARD—CARTE POSTALE"

THIS SIDE FOR ADDRESS ONLY

Buyers of picture postcards could visit a specialized store in the largest cities. This ca. 1905 view shows the Souvenir Post-Card Shop in Cleveland's down-town Colonial Arcade. *(H. Roger Grant)*

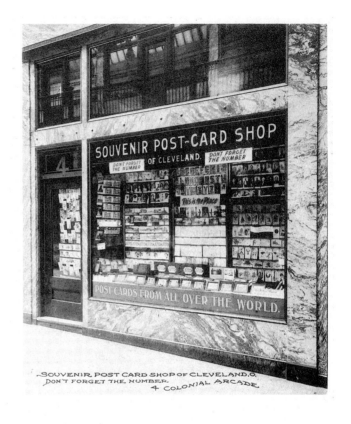

COLLINWOOD SCHOOL, after the Fire, where 174 Children lost their Lives March 4th, 1908. ERIE BOOK & POST CARD CO., CLEVELAND, O.

Picture postcards of disaster scenes are common. Cleveland-area residents eagerly acquired this view of the Collinwood School fire of March 4, 1908, in which 172 children and two teachers died. *(H. Roger Grant)*

WRECK ON THE T & O C
SEPTEMBER 14 TH, 1908 .

A less serious event took place later in 1908 when a freight and passenger train of the Toledo & Ohio Central Railroad collided near Sycamore in Wyandot County. *(H. Roger Grant)*

The tragedy at Brinkhaven, Knox County, was likely caused by the flooding of
the Mohican River during the torrential rains of Easter week 1913.
(H. Roger Grant)

Two superb examples of personalized real-photo cards are these that show the Wyandot County village of Nevada and a portrait of two women. The one mailed on August 15, 1908 *(above)*, contains this message: "This is a picture I took from our wind-mill, looking east." The other *(opposite)*, sent from Cleveland on November 10, 1906, in part notes: "I am here for a few days and had these pictures taken with Mrs. Buck. I think they are very good considering originals." *(H. Roger Grant)*

Cleveland, O.

My Dear Susie.

I am here for a few days and had these pictures taken with Mrs. Buck. I think they are very good considering originals I think perhaps I will be here Thanksgiving but will manage to see you before you return to college. Lovingly cousin Maude

Residents of Wooster, seat of Wayne County, probably reached for this "booster" postcard that celebrates their hometown. *(Claibourne E. Griffin)*

The hopes of Clevelanders to reach a million in population by 1920 is the subject
of this card produced by the city's Pitt Publishing Company.
(Claibourne E. Griffin)

Postcard Album

Ohio Landscapes

Although Ohio lacks the physical diversity of, say, California or even Georgia, the natural features of the state are varied and range from the Lake Plains in the north and the Allegheny Plateau in the southeast to the Till Plains in the west. Even without such spectacular sites as Yosemite Falls or Stone Mountain, makers of picture postcards in the Buckeye State nevertheless found interesting aspects of the natural setting, ranging from the glacial grooves on Kelleys Island in Lake Erie to the scenery along the meandering Ohio River.

The state's artificial, or "man-made," landscape also offered an array of photographic opportunities. By 1910 the larger communities had taken on an "up-to-date" appearance, and remnants of the frontier period were not always readily recognizable. The natural landscape had been altered by more than urban builders. Generations of farmers had done much to convert vast sections of wilderness into productive acres. Transportation makers, too, had left their indelible marks.

Portions of the antebellum canals remained operational until 1913, and electric and steam railroads criss-crossed the state. With the advent of the bicycle and most of all the automobile, additional miles of public roadways laced the state, beginning the process whereby internal combustion transport radically altered the physical character of the Buckeye State.

The Pebble Rocks and Chesterland Caves southeast of Cleveland prompted a postcard writer on September 1, 1909, to comment: "Visit[ed] this place today[,] a very pretty place." *(H. Roger Grant)*

Paradise Cave, located on South Bass Island in Lake Erie, offered visitors early in the century an opportunity to view stalactites and stalagmites and even a subterranean lake. *(Claibourne E. Griffin)*

The Mohican River near Greer in Knox County cuts through "Alum Rocks"
creating a picturesque scene. *(H. Roger Grant)*

The "Little Falls" on Tinker's Creek in the Cuyahoga County community of Bedford was a popular postcard view. *(H. Roger Grant)*

X 868 The Falls   Bedford O

A genuine natural Indian mound. In the heart of the city.

Native Americans constructed thousands of burial mounds throughout Ohio. The focal point of Mound Cemetery in Marietta is the well-preserved Conus Mound, named by early European American settlers. *(H. Roger Grant)*

The somnolent village of Fredericksburg is surrounded by the rolling farm land
of southern Wayne County. This view, taken in 1906, looks eastward.
(H. Roger Grant)

Looking down the Canal, Akron, O.

Brother Will be home Sunday night. Sister

Although a booming industrial city and seat of Summit County, Akron offered some appealing scenery. The Ohio and Erie Canal crossed Akron between its hills and, near the downtown, went under the massive railroad trestle of the Northern Ohio Railway. *(H. Roger Grant)*

A bridge of the Cleveland, Akron & Columbus Railroad, part of the
Pennsylvania System, and a covered wagon bridge span the Walhonding River in
western Coshocton County. *(H. Roger Grant)*

The sweeping vistas of the Muskingum River Valley reveal an assortment of tidy and presumably prosperous farms. Some of the most fertile lands in southeastern Ohio are on the floodplains of local streams. *(Claibourne E. Griffin)*

8748 Maple Leaf Inn Flower Beds Gates Mills O

Ohioans raised more than field crops; they planted countless vegetable and flower gardens. The flower beds of the Maple Leaf Inn in Gates Mills, near Cleveland, are captured in this ca. 1910 real photo card. *(H. Roger Grant)*

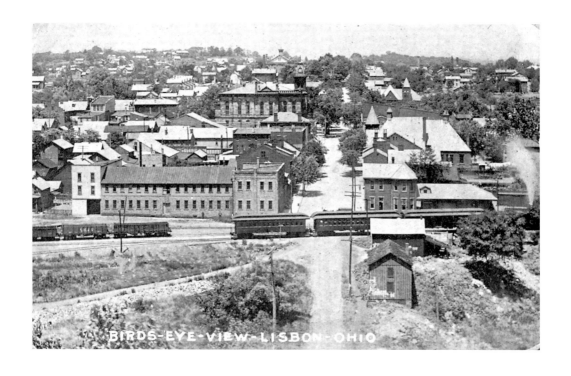

BIRDS-EYE-VIEW-LISBON-OHIO

This "bird's eye" view of Lisbon, seat of Columbiana County, dates from 1903, the year of the town's centennial. The railroad corridor, served by the Erie and Pittsburgh, Lisbon & Western Railroads, hugs the banks of Beaver Creek and the former Sandy & Beaver Canal and is overlooked on the north by commercial and residential structures. *(H. Roger Grant)*

From St. Paul's Church Spire, Delaware, Ohio.

An ambitious photographer used the spire of St. Paul's Church in Delaware to
make a panoramic view of this thriving mid-Ohio community.
(Claibourne E. Griffin)

Modest frame structures line a hilly dirt road in the Medina County village of Hinckley. *(H. Roger Grant)*

BIRD'S EYE VIEW   4-20-10   JUNCTION CITY O 1910

The rolling countryside of western Perry County is cluttered with an array of the mostly wooden buildings of Junction City and by nearly a dozen oil derricks.
(H. Roger Grant)

The rough terrain along
the Ohio River prompted
road builders to tunnel
through a hill in Ironton.
(H. Roger Grant)

Park Avenue Tunnell,
leading out of Ironton, Ohio.

Ohioans encountered mostly modest-sized rivers within their state, including the Scioto River near Hilliard in Franklin County. The Hayden Falls Bridge is typical of the iron and steel spans of the era. *(H. Roger Grant)*

The Old Mill and Ohio Canal, Zoar, Ohio.

On a lazy summer day men and women gather to fish and enjoy the surroundings of the Ohio & Erie Canal at the former utopian commune of Zoar in Tuscarawas County. *(H. Roger Grant)*

This Ohio City, Van Wert County, streetscape reveals a mostly unimproved main street, a collection of brick commercial buildings, a few trees, and a windmill. *(H. Roger Grant)*

High Street north from State St. showing electric light arches, COLUMBUS, O.

Differing from Ohio's small communities, Columbus boasts modern electric-light arches along a principal thoroughfare. This picture postcard captures a section of the capital city's north-south artery, High Street.

(H. Roger Grant)

MAIN STREET AFTER NIGHT — MANSFIELD, O.

Columbus is not the only city to display impressive electric-light arches. Mansfield residents surely took pleasure when a blaze of bulbs illuminated Main Street. *(Claibourne E. Griffin)*

The urban landscape of the early twentieth century is nicely typified by this Mt. Vernon South Main Street scene, where the automobile, electric trolley, and horse and buggy share space. *(H. Roger Grant)*

SOUTH MAIN STREET LOOKING NORTH.
AKRON, OHIO, U. S. A.

Akron's and other large communities' downtown streets were filled with an assortment of vehicles, including the electric trolley. Telephone and electric lines and poles add to the jumble of the urban landscape. *(H. Roger Grant)*

Sidewalks connect the homes along South Main Street with the commercial
heart of Clyde in Sandusky County. *(Claibourne E. Griffin)*

North Street, Ostrander, Ohio.

Quiet prevails along North Street in the Delaware County village of Ostrander,
where a mixture of commercial buildings and residences line the roadway.
(Claibourne E. Griffin)

WARWICK OHIO

Railroad corridors are an important part of the artificial landscape. Warwick, a strategic rail junction southwest of Akron, is dominated by such transportation accouterments as a frame combination-style depot, an interlocking tower, and signal masts. *(H. Roger Grant)*

EAST MAIN ST FROM THE TRACTION DEPOT · BELMORE, O

Belmore represents the small country trading centers of the turn of the century. This Putnam County village enjoyed the services of both an electric interurban and a steam railroad. Telephone poles, a bakery sign, and a railroad "cross-buck" adorn the streetscape. *(H. Roger Grant)*

OBERLIN, Ohio 1909

Seasonal changes affected streetscapes. A winter storm in 1909 coats trees and wires in Oberlin, Lorain County, with snow and ice. *(H. Roger Grant)*

Houses of mixed architectural styles commonly make up Ohio communities, whether a Queen Anne in Bedford *(above),* a colonial in Lebanon *(overleaf),* or an Arts and Crafts in Cincinnati *(page 69). (H. Roger Grant & Claibourne E. Griffin)*

GO-SA-EM-RO.

212 Wright Avenue,
Floraville,
Lebanon, Ohio.

Dear Gertrude: I want you to come Monday. Frank said he will meet you in Dayton then and see that you get here safely. He will make further arrangements with you. This is a picture of where you are coming I Till then Goodbye —
Roberta M.

Series B. 15.
Architects:
FASSE & REED,
Cincinnati, O.

ASBESTOS "CENTURY" SHINGLES
Applied French Method on the roof and Honey-comb
effect on the sides of the Residence of W. E. Crawford,
Wabash, Av., Cincinnati, O.

Contractors:
BRYEN, VANE & ANDERSON,
Cincinnati, O

Commercial Structures

In the years between the depression of the 1890s and the Great War, commercial streetscapes in Ohio continued to change, some impressively. The central cores of major cities were being rebuilt; older, smaller brick and frame structures gave way to more imposing edifices. Structural steel, electric elevators, and creative architects contributed to striking skylines.

Smaller communities evolved as well. More commercial brick buildings, or "brick blocks," often named for the owner or builder, appeared, thus extending a betterment process that had been ongoing for decades. Perhaps a fire or storm had hastened the upgrading; but the widespread prosperity made investments in commercial real estate possible. Also, incentives existed for construction of new or replacement structures. Modern, attractive places of business were good advertisements, surely encouraging customers to enter these emporiums. And bigger and better buildings, which were usually multistoried, offered opportunities for rental income from upstairs offices and apartments. Not to be overlooked was the likelihood of lower fire insurance rates because of brick and "slow burn" wood or steel superstructures.

Ohio still possessed a large number of modest frame commercial buildings. Not every place bustled; older structures remained serviceable, and if new construction occurred it was largely inexpensive. Practical Ohioans were not about to waste money on fancy "brick blocks" in sleepy cross-road villages.

Early twentieth-century commercial structures, whether modern or not, might have provided space for new types of businesses. This was a time when enterprises appeared on Main Street to sell and service automobiles, electrical products, and other advanced or replacement technologies. Communities wanted to be up-to-date, and residents wished to have picture postcards to indicate their links with modern America.

Residents of the Harrison County village of Freeport could patronize a central wooden commercial building that housed both "J. R. Hayes Groceries" and "McFadden's Restaurant." Probably employees and customers gathered for this postcard shot taken by Harbaugh's in Canal Dover. *(Claibourne E. Griffin)*

Blacksmiths C. A. Boling & Sons, in their simple false-front frame building in Creston, Wayne County, cater to the owners of automobiles by servicing rubber tires. *(H. Roger Grant)*

While the Medina Electric Light Company advertises electrical supplies,
products of the new "Age of Electricity," hitching posts, representing a fading
era, still stand at curbside. *(H. Roger Grant)*

The Highland County town of Greenfield possesses some substantial brick
commercial buildings. Harper House, which contains office and retail space in
addition to upper-story hotel rooms, commands a prime corner location.
(Claibourne E. Griffin)

726   THE CAMBRIAN HOTEL, Jackson, O.
            PUBL. BY ALEXANDER'S BOOKSTORE. JACKSON, O.

Every Ohio community of note had at least one hotel. Visitors to Jackson, seat
of Jackson County and a center of Welsh settlement, could stay in the
architecturally pleasing Cambrian Hotel. This card, mailed in 1905, predates the
use of a "split-back" for messages, so the sender wrote on the front.
(Claibourne E. Griffin)

Travelers to the east-central Ohio villages of Walhonding and Warsaw might spend their nights in the modest Nacirema *(above)* or Commercial *(opposite)* Hotels. The former features a "sanitarium" and the later provides barber services; both surely contain a dining room. *(H. Roger Grant & Claibourne E. Griffin)*

While small-town hotels were generally of mixed construction, with the better ones usually of brick or block, larger communities boasted hotels made of fire-proof materials, such as Cleveland's Hollenden House. Tall and massive edifices began to appear with the development of electric elevators and improvements in building materials, especially steel and "slow-burn" wood.

(H. Roger Grant)

Hotels were not the only well-constructed commercial structures. Banks, too, were nearly always of brick or block, as money and safe-deposit vaults required a secure and fire-proof environment. Image was also important: a solid structure meant a solid bank, important to customers before government insurance of deposits. These factors surely account for why organizers of the Kinsman Banking Company of Kinsman in Trumbull County selected brick materials.
(H. Roger Grant)

Common to the time period, professionals' offices and meeting rooms for fraternal groups took up space on upper floors. In this case, the People's National Bank in Wapakeneta occupies the ground floor of a downtown three-story commercial building; C. L. Smith, an attorney, might be found on the second floor and the Fraternal Order of Elks on the third. *(H. Roger Grant)*

MONROE BANK.
WOODSFIELD. OHIO.

The Monroe Bank towers over other buildings in Woodsfield, Monroe County's seat. With its brick and stone construction, columns, and architectural detail, this edifice suggests strength and stability. *(Claibourne E. Griffin)*

Public Buildings

From the time of the Northwest Territory, Ohioans have shown interest in their public buildings, particularly in their county court houses. These structures engendered considerable civic pride and frequently dominated the local landscape, especially in those communities that used the town-square plan. It was common for a county seat to have seen several court houses. Often the initial frame or brick building, perhaps of classical styling, gave way in the post–Civil War era to a larger and more substantial edifice. Growth demanded it. When confronted with the need to modernize, representatives of county governments commonly preferred styles that reflected popular Victorian tastes. Then in the early twentieth century additional replacement structures appeared to accommodate expanding county government. Fires, too—open-flame heating and lighting systems might be the evil culprits—sometimes prompted replacement.

Should an Ohio community fail to achieve county-seat status, residents could still take pride in a municipal hall. While these buildings usually lacked the size and architectural elegance of a court house, they were more than merely flimsy frame structures. And in the early twentieth century, residents often found it necessary to replace or expand these buildings because of population growth.

By the First World War larger Ohio communities, whether seats of county government or not, usually had a variety of appealing public buildings, either new or remodeled, including post offices, fire stations, libraries, hospitals, and fraternal or related structures. After all, this was the time of urban expansion, increased public expenditures on capital improvements, and acts of private philanthropy, best represented by Andrew Carnegie's funding of library projects.

Ohio also possessed its share of lowly public buildings. A village might have a post office attached to a general store or a volunteer fire company housed in a large shed. Township halls might resemble rural schools.

No matter the size or style, a vast assortment of public buildings could be found in the Buckeye State in the early part of the century, and many of these structures were ideally suited for the picture postcard entrepreneur.

If any building during the Golden Age of picture postcards represents Ohio, it is the Statehouse. An outstanding example of the Greek Revival style, this large Doric structure stands in downtown Columbus and dates from the antebellum years. The cornerstone was laid in 1839, and although some departments occupied the building in 1857, it was not completed until 1861. *(H. Roger Grant)*

STATE CAPITOL, COLUMBUS, OHIO

Cincinnati O. 11.17. '05. You see I am still here. I wanted to be home for Lily's birthday Sunday but here I must stay for a while longer. Can you find me?

Hope you are well Love to you both,

Government Building. Cincinnati, Ohio

How do you like the Cincinnati cards?
No. 447 Published by The Cincinnati News Company, Cincinnati, Ohio–Leipzig–Berlin.
4165. Apple st. n. side. Mrs. J. B. Candy.

The federal government constructed some substantial public structures, including Cincinnati's "Government Building," an architectural gem from the Gilded Age that covers a downtown city block. *(H. Roger Grant)*

After the Civil War, the taxpayers of Richland County financed a stylish courthouse and jail in Mansfield. Several Ohio counties opted for jails that, in addition to cells, provided living quarters for the sheriff and his family. Such apartments meant that the building was always occupied, and the sheriff's wife could also earn extra income by cooking meals for prisoners. *(H. Roger Grant)*

The Washington County
Courthouse, with its im-
pressive clock tower,
dominates the skyline of
Marietta. *(Claibourne E.
Griffin)*

Wash. Co. Court House, Marietta, O.

Old Court House, Painesville, Ohio

As Ohio's population increased, so did the need for the services of county governments. Original or early courthouses usually required replacement or were considered outdated by the late nineteenth and early twentieth centuries, as was the case in Painesville, Lake County, where the nineteenth-century Greek Revival courthouse was already called the "Old Court House" in 1910.
(H. Roger Grant)

Courthouses became popu-
lar gathering places in all of
the eighty-eight county seat
communities, as reflected in
this postcard of the Knox
County courthouse in Mt.
Vernon, which also shows
the architectural tastes of
the nineteenth century.
(H. Roger Grant)

4639   Court House, Mt. Vernon, O.

The larger and more prosperous counties usually erected substantial courthouses. One example is in Newark, the Licking County seat. This view card, published by the Rotograph Company of New York and printed in Germany, shows that Newark had become an important place, in fact a center for production of such products as glassware and stoves. *(Claibourne E. Griffin)*

A 4502 County Court House, Newark, O.

CITY HALL OSNABURG, O.

The village of Osnaburg, founded in 1805 and renamed East Canton during the
anti-German hysteria of the First World War, built a multipurpose "City Hall"
with space for municipal offices and fire-fighting equipment.
(Claibourne E. Griffin)

LINTON, TP, HOUSE.

PLAINFIELD O.

The seat of township life in the village of Plainfield, Coshocton County, is accommodated in a spartan two-story frame structure that is somewhat enhanced by a bell tower. Local units of government usually used inexpensive buildings of wooden construction. *(H. Roger Grant)*

Mansfield's post office *(right)* and public library *(opposite)* are solid buildings of cut stone. The Romanesque styling of the library made for an especially attractive edifice. *(H. Roger Grant)*

The Post Office — Mansfield, Ohio.

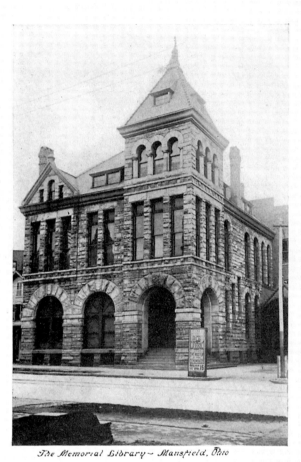

The Memorial Library ~ Mansfield, Ohio

The post office in Amesville, Athens County, situated in the Hocking Valley coal
fields, takes over the ground floor of the Knights of Pythias building, just as the
Mansfield post office uses the street-level of the Masonic Temple.
(Claibourne E. Griffin)

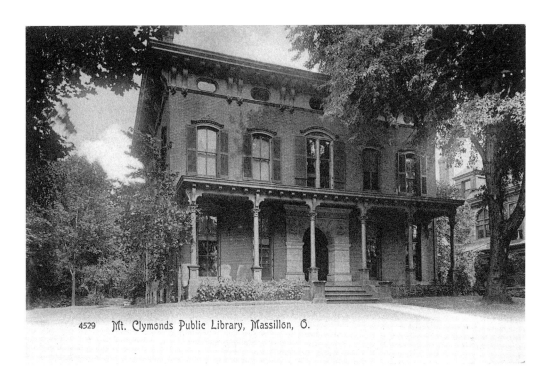

4529   Mt. Clymonds Public Library, Massillon, O.

The Mt. Clymonds Public Library in Massillon utilizes space in a former
residence of Italianate design. *(H. Roger Grant)*

Public Library, Clyde, Ohio.

Residents of Clyde surely took civic pride in their unusual public library, which
resembles a collegiate facility more than a small-town library.
(Claibourne E. Griffin)

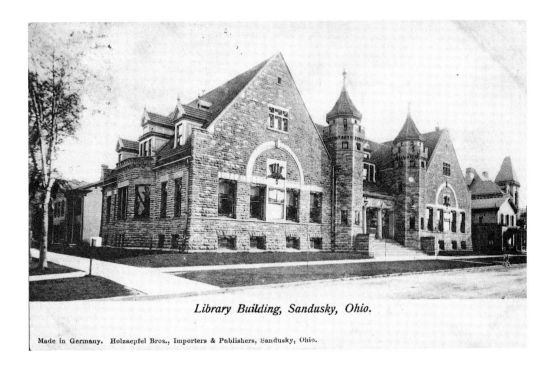

Library Building, Sandusky, Ohio.

Made in Germany. Holzaepfel Bros., Importers & Publishers, Sandusky, Ohio.

Just as Clyde residents presumably admired (and doubtless patronized) their library, the one available to readers in nearby Sandusky is even more imposing.
(Claibourne E. Griffin)

St. Francis' Hospital. Columbus, Ohio

While extensive library construction occurred during the late nineteenth and early twentieth centuries, hospitals also blossomed. Population growth and better medical treatments necessitated new or expanded facilities. The St. Francis Hospital was built to help meet the medical needs of Columbus.
(H. Roger Grant)

Small Ohio communities required more modest facilities for treating the sick. Private homes might be converted into hospitals or sanitariums. One example can be found in this facility that serves residents of Millersburg and the surrounding area of Holmes County. *(Claibourne E. Griffin)*

SANITARIUM, MILLERSBURG, OHIO.

A public building might offer multiple uses. Just as Osnaburg has a combination townhall and fire station, Jefferson, the seat of Ashtabula County, in 1900 saw construction of a dual fire station and public library. *(H. Roger Grant)*

The Young Men's Christian Association, started nationally in the early 1870s, sponsored special "Railroad Y's," which offered clean, safe, and inexpensive rooms. By the early twentieth century, the organization operated nearly 180 hotels that catered to railroaders, including this one for employees of the "Big Four" Railroad at Linndale (Gresham), near Cleveland. *(H. Roger Grant)*

HAVE YOU SEEN OUR NEW BUILDING?

DO YOU WISH TO SEE THE NEW CLASS ROOMS, LIBRARY AND GYMNASIUM?

DO YOU WISH TO SHARE IN THE GOOD THINGS OFFERED HERE TO YOUNG WOMEN?

DO YOU WISH TO ENTER A CLASS?

COME TO THE
CLASS RALLY
THURSDAY EVE., SEPT. 19

REGISTRATION DAYS, SEPT. 19, 20 AND 21

THE CLEVELAND Y. W. C. A. BUILDING
PROSPECT AVE. AND E. 18TH ST. S. E.

An illustration of a larger and more publicly oriented Y is the building housing the Cleveland Young Women's Christian Association. *(Claibourne E. Griffin)*

Buildings erected by fraternal organizations also
offered quasi-public func-
tions. The structure usually
had commercial outlets on
the ground floor, office
space in other sections, and
a great hall that not only
served the order's needs
but also could be used for
public meetings and recep-
tions. The Masonic Temple
in Zanesville represents
architectural tastes of the
turn of the century.
(H. Roger Grant)

MASONIC TEMPLE. ZANESVILLE, O.

Monuments and Memorials

By the Golden Age of picture postcards, a rich variety of monuments and memorials had become part of the Ohio landscape. These objects made for popular photographic subjects and became a staple of locally oriented cards. Throughout the state and nation there existed a long-standing desire to have specially designated or designed artifacts to remind citizens of their historical heritage, tell their ideals, and suggest goals toward which they should strive.

The character of monuments and memorials in Ohio varied. They might be buildings, cannons, or even trees. Some were fashioned for particular reasons. Probably the most popular monuments and memorials were statues commemorating military deeds, often associated with the bloody Civil War. Although the Buckeye State lacked anything as spectacular as the Washington National Monument, dedicated in 1885 and located in the nation's capital, Ohio was home to some impressive monuments and memorials. Two illustrations of the genre included the James A.

Garfield Monument, a circular tower 50 feet in diameter and 180 feet high, which in 1890 became a focal point of Cleveland's Lake View Cemetery, and the Zane-Kenton Memorial, a sixty-ton boulder surrounded by forged iron chairs, which honored pioneers Isaac Zane and Simon Kenton and was dedicated in 1914 in the Logan County village of Zanesfield.

My Jewels Monument, located on the northwest corner of the Statehouse in Columbus, features bronze statues of Salmon Chase, James Garfield, Ulysses Grant, Rutherford Hayes, Philip Sheridan, William Sherman, and Edwin Stanton that stand on a granite pedestal. The representations surround a shaft topped by a statue of Cornelia, the Roman matron. Her words, "These Are My Jewels," stand out in relief at the top of the column. The Civil War–inspired monument, the artistic creation of Levi Scofield, was exhibited by the state at the World's Columbian Exposition in Chicago in 1893 and later placed on the capitol grounds. *(H. Roger Grant)*

Ohio's Jewels -- Columbus.

A stylized statue of an Indian rests atop the Harris monument in the Medina County community of Lodi. Judge Joseph Harris helped found the town, and a writer on the back of this picture postcard explains that "The Harris people were among the first settlers here in what is Lodi now, and these Indians [were] here then. Their descendants [Harrises] still live here. This momument [*sic*] is down in the park." *(Claibourne E. Griffin)*

West High St and Public Square
Mt Vernon, O

As a response to a strong desire to memorialize the victims of the costliest war in American history, Civil War monuments became popular features of public parks and squares. Approximately 35,000 Ohioans died, about 11,000 from battle wounds and the remainder from disease. This card shows the Civil War memorial in Mt. Vernon. *(H. Roger Grant)*

SOLDIER'S MONUMENT WILMOT O.

Residents of even small communities erected a "Soldier's Monument" to the "Memory of the Soldiers of the Civil War." A Canal Dover photographer made this picture postcard not long after this monument was placed in the Wilmot, Stark County, cemetery in 1908. *(H. Roger Grant)*

Ashlanders, too, expressed their gratitude to the Civil War dead. The inscription reads: "Erected by Mr. and Mrs. Jonas Freer to the Memory of Our Dead Soldiers 1888." The local Andrews Post of the Grand Army of Republic, the Union army veterans group, contributed a fully equipped artillery piece to the monument site. *(H. Roger Grant)*

SOLDIERS' MONUMENT- ASHLAND, O.

About 1910 the Grand Army of the Republic erected a temporary "Court of Honor" on Public Square in Lima. *(Claibourne E. Griffin)*

THE LIVING FLAG G.A.R. ENCAMPMENT TOLEDO, O. 08, T-18
POST CARD Co BRYAN, O.

The Grand Army of Republic sponsored annual state encampments from the 1880s until the 1920s, including this one held during September 1908 in Toledo. Participants, who were mostly veterans and their wives, made a "living flag," likely a high point of the festivities. *(Claibourne E. Griffin)*

MAUSOLEUM ON
DECORATION DAY

LONGENBAKER PHOTO

On July 13, 1913, Greenville, the Darke County seat, dedicated a mausoleum—
a major community event. The public was invited to "Come and bring your
friends and inspect this Marble Palace." *(Claibourne E. Griffin)*

About 1910 "Decoration Day," later Memorial Day, drew a crowd and the village brass band to the public square in the Geauga County village of Parkman.
(Claibourne E. Griffin)

Elk's Memorial in Green Lawn Cemetery

In a picture postcard series sponsored about 1905 by the *Columbus Dispatch,* one view shows the dedication of the Fraternal Order of Elks' memorial in the local Green Lawn Cemetery. *(H. Roger Grant)*

Birth Place of Ex-President Hayes, Delaware, O.

Ohioans were proud of the several native sons who became presidents of the United States. Delaware proudly sold a commemorative card that honored the nation's nineteenth president, Rutherford Birchard Hayes, born in that town on October 4, 1822. *(Claibourne E. Griffin)*

The assassination of President William McKinley of Canton in September 1901 prompted local card makers to honor this martyred Ohioan. This popular image of the late president was taken on his front porch, the focal point of the 1896 presidential campaign. *(Claibourne E. Griffin)*

Religion

❧ ❧ ❧

Ohio's religious fabric rapidly took shape with the arrival of the first European American settlers. The three distinct areas of early migration created patterns of religious diversity that suggested the rich mixture that was to follow. Baptists, Congregationalists, Episcopalians, Methodists, and Presbyterians came from New England to the Western Reserve in the northeast; Anabaptist and Pietist sects, Methodists, and Quakers entered the state's midsection; and Baptists, Episcopalians, Lutherans, Methodists, and Presbyterians migrated to the Virginia Military District in the south.

The pioneer Protestant denominations would not exist alone. Other groups planted themselves in Ohio and represented a multiplicity of faiths, ranging from Adventists (Millerites) to the Church of Jesus Christ of Latter-day Saints (Mormons) to the Disciples of Christ (Campbellites), as well as Jews and Roman Catholics. With the immigration of uprooted central, eastern, and southern Europeans, the Jewish population increased, and more Roman Catholics and new Eastern Orthodox parishes became conspicuous in industrial cities like Cleveland, Toledo, and Youngstown. Recently formed indigenous sects also appeared, including those associated with the New Thought Movement of the late nineteenth century. The most popular churches belonged to disciples of Mary Baker Eddy, discoverer and founder of Christian Science.

In the early twentieth century the nature of religion in Ohio mirrored national patterns. The largest religious organization in the state, the Roman Catholic Church, recorded 843,856 parishioners. As in many states, Methodists held the honor of being the Protestant body with the largest Ohio membership. At this time the followers of John Wesley belonged to two principal units, the Methodist Episcopal Church (with bishops) and the Methodist Protestant Church (without bishops). Also, several black Methodist bodies functioned in the state, the African Methodist Episcopal Church being the largest. The Bureau of the Census's *Religious Bodies 1916* reported that of the 2,291,793 Ohioans who named a particular denomination, Methodist groups counted 435,823 members. The next largest Protestant denomination, the Presbyterians, claimed 160,413 adherents.

Church buildings, without regard to denomination, frequently became the objects of much pride. Understandably, a good market existed for church and religious-related picture postcards.

United Brethern.

Methodist Episcopal.

St. Clement's Roman Catholic.

Churches of Navarre, Ohio, U. S. A.

. St. Paul's Evangelical.

The Old Brick Church.

Navarre, a Stark County village, is representative of Ohio's religious diversity, including churches of Ohio's two largest Christian communions, Roman Catholics and Methodists. *(Claibourne E. Griffin)*

SACRED HEART CHURCH NEW PHILA. O.

Sacred Heart Church in New Philadelphia once housed a Lutheran congregation. On the message side, the writer comments: "It [the church] looks small but it is larger than it looks." *(Claibourne E. Griffin)*

Sacred Heart Seminary
Shelby, Ohio

A Roman Catholic order operates the Sacred Heart Seminary in the Richland County town of Shelby. By the early twentieth century Ohio had a well-established tradition of Catholic-sponsored education. *(Claibourne E. Griffin)*

BISHOP KOUDELKA AT NEW CHURCH OF OUR LADY OF CONSOLATION. CAREY. OHIO.

A procession of Roman Catholic clerics passes the foundation of the soon-to-be built Our Lady of Consolation Church in the Wyandot County town of Carey. Nearby is the Shrine of Our Lady of Consolation, established in 1875 by a Luxembourg-born priest. *(Claibourne E. Griffin)*

One of Ohio's most famous church buildings is the First Methodist Church in Canton. William McKinley and his wife, Ida, attended this church and it was here in September 1901 that the funeral for the slain president took place. Shortly after the interment of her husband, Mrs. McKinley presented the congregation with four stained-glass windows portraying her favorite biblical characters. *(H. Roger Grant)*

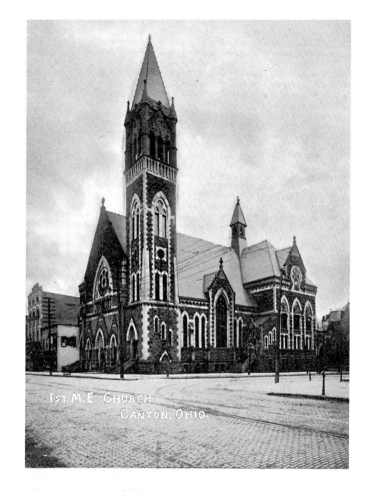

1st. M.E. Church
Canton, Ohio.

M. E. Church, Prairie Depot, Ohio

It has been suggested that at the turn of the century the state's Republican party had as its fraternal arm the Grand Army of the Republic and as its religious arm the Methodist church, as seen here with the placement of a Civil War memorial next to the Methodist church in the Wood County village of Prairie Depot.
(Claibourne E. Griffin)

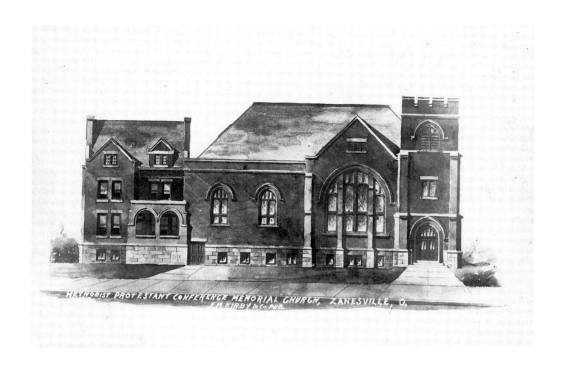

Methodist Protestant Conference Memorial Church, Zanesville, O.
F.H. Kirby & Co. Pub.

Although Methodists claimed the largest membership among Ohio Protestants at this time, the denomination consisted of several splinter groups, including the Methodist Protestants, whose new church in Zanesville appears on this picture postcard made about 1910. *(Claibourne E. Griffin)*

Ohio churches often provided housing for their ministers or priests, an example being this new, impressive Methodist parsonage in the village of Harpster in Wyandot County. *(H. Roger Grant)*

Baptists dominated the religious life of the Licking County community of Granville, where the church served townspeople and as well as those associated with the nearby Baptist-affiliated Denison University. *(Claibourne E. Griffin)*

The tidy German Reformed church and its parsonage, built in 1898, stand in the Stark County village of Hartville. *(H. Roger Grant)*

THE L. D. S. TEMPLE
Kirtland, Ohio

A nationally famous church building is the Mormon Temple in Kirtland, east of Cleveland. Between 1833 and 1836 followers of Joseph Smith, Jr., founder of this distinctly American faith, labored with inspired energy and religiosity to create this structure of mixed Georgian, Gothic, Greek, Egyptian, and Venetian motifs. *(H. Roger Grant)*

SPIRIT FRUIT FARM.

The "Incubator" of the "Spirit Fruit Religion." Spirit Fruit Society was founded in 1901 by Jacob L. Beilhart and was removed to Ingleside, Ill. in 1905.

During the Golden Age of picture postcards, only a few utopian experiments were active in Ohio. One commune was the Spirit Fruit Society, which was founded officially in 1901 by Jacob Beilhart and was an eclectic blend of Christianity and theosophy. The Society acquired a small farm on the north side of Lisbon and settled into a peaceful and industrious, if morally unorthodox, way of life. But subsequent troubles with some local residents over "free love" prompted the Society to leave for Illinois in 1904. *(H. Roger Grant)*

The Dr. French E. Oliver Tabernacle, Findlay, Ohio
Published by S. H. Knox & Co.

FINDLAY FOR CHRIST

For Ohioans attracted to independent, fundamentalist groups, flimsy, albeit
large, frame structures or tents adequately served for revivals and meetings, as
seen in this ca. 1910 postcard of the Dr. French E. Oliver Tabernacle in Findlay.
(Claibourne E. Griffin)

Our Father was a United Brethren Preacher. We are at Otterbein Home.

This poignant portrait of the widow and four children of a United Brethren pastor suggests that the family lives in the Otterbein Home in Westerville, northeast of Columbus, where the United Brethren–sponsored Otterbein College is located. *(Claibourne E. Griffin)*

Church groups used picture postcards to promote special events, like the
twenty-sixth annual Christian Endeavor gathering in Cleveland in 1911 *(above)*
and the First Reformed Church's "Rally Day Services" in Canton in 1913
(overleaf). (Claibourne E. Griffin)

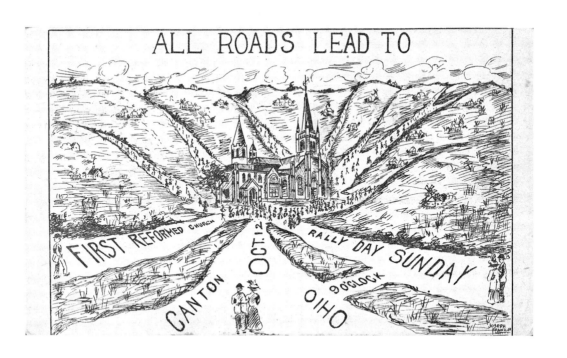

Education

As the twentieth century developed, residents of Ohio could take pride in the abundance of educational opportunities. By 1914, for example, the state possessed 798 public high schools; only Pennsylvania could claim more. The future looked bright for the tens of thousands of school-aged children. Their chances of having twelve rather than eight or fewer years of schooling had significantly increased.

The nature of education in Ohio, however, was in transition. Although as late as 1914 the state had nearly ten thousand one-room schoolhouses, for generations the symbol of public education, the move was underway to replace them with "centralized" or "consolidated" facilities. Similarly, private academies, frequently tied to a religious denomination, closed their doors as better public institutions opened. With educational restructuring and continued population growth, new grammar, intermediate, and high schools became common. These structures, often of brick construction, contemporary design, and practical floor plans, emerged as new badges of progressive education in the Buckeye State.

Ohio's system of higher education also changed and readily grew to serve the constituency. In 1914 the state ranked second (after Pennsylvania) in the number of colleges, universities, and schools of technology, with forty such institutions scattered throughout the state. Church-related colleges were the most numerous; Methodists, Presbyterians, and Roman Catholics had been especially energetic in college building. During the early part of the century, the interest in better teacher-training also helped alter public education. In 1902 the General Assembly provided for a state-supported teacher school in connection with Miami and Ohio Universities and five years later established one at Ohio State University. Then in 1910 lawmakers created free-standing "normal," or teacher, colleges in Bowling Green and Kent. Three years later Buchtel College, founded by Universalists in 1870 and nondenominational since 1907, became the city-sponsored University of Akron, part of a national and state movement of municipal colleges which included the establishment of the University of Cincinnati and the University of Toledo. By the First World War there was some validity to the saying that "if you go into an Ohio town, you'll get a degree!"

Fulton Twp. Public School, Swanton, Ohio   School Post Card Co., Columbus, O

Drivers of horse-drawn schoolbuses are about to leave a township school in rural Fulton County. *(Claibourne E. Griffin)*

Unlike residents in other Midwestern states, Ohioans built a large number of brick rural schools, such as this one near Corsica in central Ohio.
(Claibourne E. Griffin)

Before the great wave of school consolidations, smaller communities might support privately operated academies, as Ashtabula County's village of New Lyme was home to the New Lyme Institute. *(Claibourne E. Griffin)*

New Lyme Institute

An endowed college preparatory school.

Music, Manual Training, Domestic Science, Land and Railroad Surveying and Mechanical Drawing are among the electives.

First Semester of 1912-13 commences on the first Tuesday of Sept. This school will be found very attractive to students who have not yet decided to prepare for college. For particulars address

Pres. Alfred E. Gladding, A. M.
NEW LYME, OHIO.

In Danville, Knox County, most, if not all, of the students gather informally for this picture in front of their modern multistory brick "public school."

(H. Roger Grant)

The old and new high schools of Bedford appear in this ca. 1907 view card.
(H. Roger Grant)

Copyright 1905 by the Rotograph Co.

11903   Main Building, Ohio State University, Columbus, O.

The Ohio State University in Columbus distributed this picture postcard *(above)*
of University Hall with a list of requirements for admission printed on the back
(opposite). (Claibourne E. Griffin)

REQUIREMENTS FOR ADMISSION to the OHIO STATE UNIVERSITY.

SUBJECTS	BRANCHES	Value in Units	College of Agric. and Dom. Sci.	College of Arts, Phil. and Sci.	College of Engineering	College of Law	College of Pharmacy
English	Composition and Rhetoric	1					1
	Classics	1	2	2	2	2	1
	Literature	1					
History	Civil Government	½					½
	U. S. History	½					½
	General History	1	2	2	2	2	1
	Greek and Roman History	½ or 1					
	English History	1					
Mathematics	Algebra, through quad.	1	1		1		1
	Algebra, beyond quad.	½			½		½
	Plane Geometry	1	1	3	1	3	1
	Solid Geometry	½			½		½
	Plane Trigonometry	½					
Language	Latin	2 to 4	4 (2 units may be elected from other groups.)	6 (2 units may be elected from other groups.)	6 (2 units may be elected from other groups.)	4 (2 units may be elected from other groups.)	2 or 2
	Greek	2 " 4					
	German	2 " 4					
	French	2 " 4					
	Spanish	2 " 4					
Science	Physics	1	1	1	1	1	1
	Physical Geography	½	½				½
	Chemistry	1					
	Botany	½	½				½
	Physiology	½					
	Zo-ology	½		1	1	1	
	Geology	½					
	Astronomy	½					
	Agriculture	½					
	Total Units Required		12	15	15	13	11

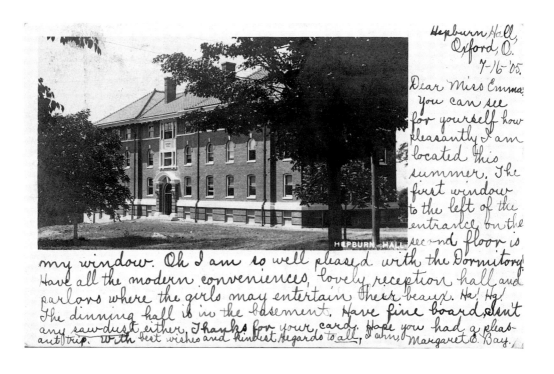

Hepburn Hall,
Oxford, O.
7-16-'05.
Dear Miss Emma:
You can see
for yourself how
pleasantly I am
located this
summer. The
first window
to the left of the
entrance on the
second floor is
my window. Oh I am so well pleased with the Dormitory!
Have all the modern conveniences, lovely reception hall and
parlors where the girls may entertain their beaux. Ha! Ha!
The dinning hall is in the basement. Have fine board. Isn't
any saw dust either. Thanks for your card. Hope you had a pleasant trip. With best wishes and kindest regards to all, I am, Margaret E. Bay.

Margaret Bay, a student at Miami University in Oxford, selected a card of her
dormitory, Hepburn Hall, about which she wrote: "Oh I am so well pleased
with the Dormitory. Have all the modern conveniences, lovely reception hall
and parlors where the girls may entertain their beaux. The dinning hall is in the
basement." *(Claibourne E. Griffin)*

Central State University, founded in 1877 in Wilberforce, in Greene County, and originally designed to train teachers, primarily served students of the state's African American population. This view card shows Galloway Hall.
(Claibourne E. Griffin)

The path that leads to Glory.

Dear Old Kenyon 10/11/06   C.H.G

A student at Kenyon College in Gambier, Knox County, penned the comment "The path that leads to Glory" on this picture postcard of an entrance to the campus "decorated" by the Class of 1901. *(H. Roger Grant)*

Jan. 19, 1906.
Many thanks for card. The hotel looks very fine.
Blanche Griswold.

Western Reserve University (Adelbert College)--Cleveland

One of Ohio's premier private institutions of higher education was Western
Reserve University in Cleveland. A building of the University's Adelbert College
for men is captured on this 1906 card. *(H. Roger Grant)*

An Akron department store, the M. O'Neil & Co., sold this view card that honors the city's private Buchtel College, which in 1913 became the Municipal University of Akron. *(Claibourne E. Griffin)*

SPRINGFIELD O

Wittenberg University students, perhaps members of a musical group, wait at a Springfield railroad station ca. 1910. The reverse side contains a predictable message from a college student: "Will be home Wednesday evening and want you to meet me at the train with the buggy because my suitcase will be awful heavy and I will have several things to carry." *(Claibourne E. Griffin)*

College presents apparently lacked luxurious offices, as this ca. 1910 picture postcard of Herbert Welch, president of Ohio Wesleyan University in Delaware, indicates. *(Claibourne E. Griffin)*

Dr. Herbert Welch, Pres. of Ohio Wesleyan University, in his Office in Univerty Hall, DELAWARE, Ohio.

Transportation

Arguably no state enjoyed better transportation than Ohio. If members of a community had missed out on the advantages of a natural or an artificial waterway, they surely received the benefits of a steam railway. By the early years of the twentieth century, Ohioans had access to more than nine thousand miles of main, secondary, and branch lines (greater mileage could be found only in Illinois, Iowa, Pennsylvania, and Texas), and towns in Ohio likely had the services of two or even more steam carriers.

In addition, residents of these places, who somehow believed that they had been unfairly dealt with by transportation promoters, received still another chance to reduce their isolation. This time the transportation form was the electric interurban railway, which had made its debut nationally near the end of the nineteenth century. Ohio witnessed one of the first intercity electric railways in the country, the Akron, Bedford & Cleveland Railroad, which opened in 1895 between the communities of its corporate name. No other state approached within a thousand miles Ohio's interurban mileage of 2,798, and no Ohio community with a population of ten thousand lacked interurban service.

Further adding to the availability of public transportation were the increased miles of improved, or "all-weather," roads that came in the wake of the bicycle craze of the 1890s and the growing love affair after 1900 with the automobile. Residents saw more construction of brick, macadam, and concrete roads. And in 1913 they applauded the formation of the Lincoln Highway Association, which soon blazed the way for the nation's first transcontinental highway (later the route of U.S. 30) and for service across the northern part of the state.

Thus, a combination of water, rail, and road transport created a lacework of avenues that effectively bound Ohio. The options for travel were impressive.

Although much of the Ohio canal system had been abandoned by the time of the picture postcard craze, some sections did remain in service, most notably the northern end of the Ohio & Erie Canal. This unidentified scene is likely from the Cleveland area, as the postcard was mailed in the Forest City on January 31, 1911. *(H. Roger Grant)*

A boat moves along the
Ohio & Erie Canal near
Bolivar in northern Tuscarawas County. The Easter
week floods of 1913 perma-
nently closed this portion of
the waterway. *(H. Roger
Grant)*

8968 Along the Ohio Canal,
Bolivar, Ohio

The deteriorating aqueduct of the Ohio & Erie Canal spans the Scioto River in Pickaway County near Circleville. *(H. Roger Grant)*

4732   At the Wharf Side, Gallipolis, O.

From the first European Americans' arrival in the Ohio Country, the Ohio River served as an artery of commerce. But by the early twentieth century, most traffic involved low-cost bulk freight and ferry service, steamboats having lost most of their business to the railroads. Yet in this ca. 1905 view card, the public wharf at Gallipolis, seat of Gallia County, still welcomes steamboats.

(Claibourne E. Griffin)

A steamboat with a "tow" of barges churns along the Ohio River near Marietta.
(Claibourne E. Griffin)

"The Lorena" on Muskingum River, Malta, Ohio

The Lorena, built in 1895 for service between Zanesville and Pittsburgh, travels the Muskingum River in Morgan County near Malta. The river was "canalized" with a series of locks and dams between Marietta and Dresden, north of Zanesville, where it meets the Ohio & Erie Canal. *(H. Roger Grant)*

CITY OF CLEVELAND
LARGEST SIDE WHEEL STEAMER ON FRESH WATER   87   PESHA PHOTO

Just as the Ohio River offered the state's residents access to large sections of the nation, the Great Lakes similarly tied them to numerous destinations. A major passenger, express, and mail carrier on Lake Erie was the Detroit & Cleveland Navigation Company. This photo card proclaims that the *City of Cleveland* is the "largest side wheel steamer on fresh water." *(H. Roger Grant)*

River Front, Penn. R. R. Docks, Toledo, Ohio.

Marie Elwell

Toledo served as a major coal and grain shipping point on the Great Lakes. This view of the harbor area reveals docks owned by the Pennsylvania Railroad.
(H. Roger Grant)

Although for decades the Pennsylvania Railroad boasted that it was the "Standard Railway of the World," the powerful Philadelphia-based carrier possessed its share of modest, standardized small-town depots like this one in Spring Valley, Greene County, on the company's Cincinnati–Columbus line.
(H. Roger Grant)

In this ca. 1910 postcard, the passenger crew of the Pennsylvania Railroad's subsidiary, the Cleveland, Akron & Columbus Railroad, waits to leave the Akron station. The locomotive is an "American Standard," a popular type assigned to passenger runs. *(H. Roger Grant)*

1912

A north-bound Cleveland, Akron & Columbus four-car passenger train is seen east of the roundhouse in Mt. Vernon. *(H. Roger Grant)*

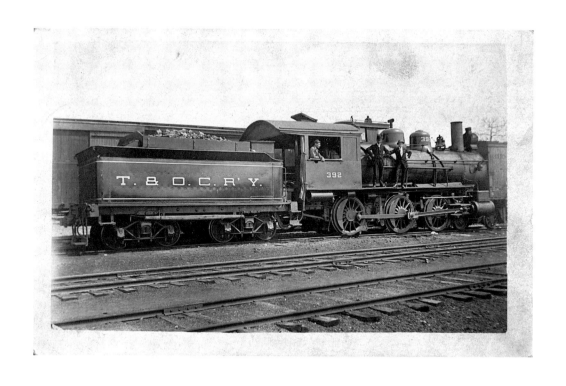

While the Pennsylvania Railroad controlled the Cleveland, Akron & Columbus, its great rival, the New York Central, controlled the Toledo & Ohio Central Railroad. This real photo card of a "Ten-Wheeler," taken in Newark, dates from May 3, 1910. *(H. Roger Grant)*

A couple of Baltimore & Ohio employees stand by two freight locomotives in the yard at Holloway, Belmont County, on the largely coal-carrying Bridgeport-Cleveland line. This card is a product of Freter Brothers, "Famous Post Cards, Made at Bridgeport, Bellaire & Martins Ferry, Ohio." *(H. Roger Grant)*

The rugged terrain of Cincinnati prompted construction of the Mount Adams Incline Plane, one of several that operated in the Queen City. *(H. Roger Grant)*

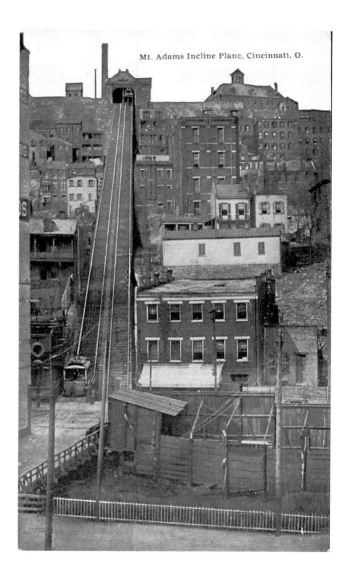

Mt. Adams Incline Plane, Cincinnati, O.

Scene on Suburban Line, running out of Cleveland

This bridge connects Cleveland Rocky River village. Come again. C. E. Anderson, Cleveland, O.

The electric trolley era began nationwide at the end of the 1880s, and by the early years of the twentieth century virtually every Ohio city and town claimed a street traction operation. Here a trolley rumbles over the Rocky River bridge west of Cleveland. *(H. Roger Grant)*

First Electric Car, Fayette, Ohio.

A red-letter day in the life of any Ohio community was the arrival of the first electric interurban car. By 1915 the state had become the heartland of long-distance, intercity electric railways. The motorman and conductor of the "First Electric Car, Fayette, Ohio," employees of the Toledo & Western Railway, happily pose for a photographer. *(H. Roger Grant)*

Residents of Plymouth, in Huron and Richland counties, gather on their public
square in 1904 to witness the arrival of their town's first interurban, the Sandusky,
Norwalk & Mansfield Electric Railway. The road initially connected Norwalk
and Plymouth (seventeen miles), and in 1907 it built an eight-mile extension to
Shelby; however, the firm never reached Sandusky or Mansfield on its own rails.
(H. Roger Grant)

Three forms of early-twentieth-century transport are displayed in this image taken near Plymouth: horse and wagon, interurban (Sandusky, Norwalk & Mansfield), and steam railroad (Baltimore & Ohio). *(H. Roger Grant)*

Beech City was served by two steam railroads, the Baltimore & Ohio and the Wheeling & Lake Erie, and also by an electric interurban, the Northern Ohio Traction & Light Company (NOT&L). In this ca. 1910 view card, one of the NOT&L's big wooden cars rolls through the commercial heart of this Stark County village. *(H. Roger Grant)*

Travelers congregate at the small frame depot of the Cincinnati & Columbus Traction Company in the Brown County community of Fayetteville. While this fifty-three mile "juice road" linked Cincinnati and Hillsboro, its promoters' plans to reach Columbus were never realized. *(H. Roger Grant)*

Richwood, a Union County town, was the terminus of a small interurban, the Columbus, Magnetic Springs & Northern Railway. In 1904 the road opened between Delaware, seat of Delaware County, and Magnetic Springs in Union County; soon thereafter the line was extended to Richwood, a station on the Erie Railroad. The backers of the electric road owned Magnetic Park in Magnetic Springs, but their hopes for the development of the town as a resort were never fulfilled, and the interurban ceased operations during the First World War. *(H. Roger Grant)*

A FLEET OF CANNING TRUCKS, BUILT BY THE GRAMM-LOGAN MOTOR CAR COMPANY OF BOWLING GREENE O, U.S.A. THE MOST SUCCESSFUL TRUCK BUILDERS IN THE WORLD, WRITE FOR CATALOG.

PUB. BY M. WEINELBAUN CO. LIMA O.

Although Ohio interurbans captured a considerable volume of short-distance passenger, express, and less-than-carload freight from their steam rivals, by the 1920s motor trucks injured, even destroyed, the freight revenues of their electric competitors. This circa 1918 view card shows a fleet of Crady Canning Company trucks built by the Gramm-Logan Motor Car Company of Bowling Green.

(*H. Roger Grant*)

It is an unhappy day in March 1915 for this Cleveland-made Winton automobile,
whose "remains of fire" were found in the Summit County village of Twinsburg.
(H. Roger Grant)

Motor cars join a few bug-
gies for some spectator
event—perhaps an auto
race—in Stark County.
(H. Roger Grant)

BRECKSVILLE - NORTH

Automobiles are hardly crowding this public road that enters Brecksville in Cuyahoga County. *(Claibourne E. Griffin)*

Industry

Once the cataclysmic depression of the 1890s had run its course, the Ohio economy rebounded dramatically. Older manufacturing plants expanded and new factories opened. Smoke filled the air, but few publicly complained—after all, heavy smoke meant prosperity and progress. And, too, the soft-coal mining industry was vital to the state's economic health. Residents adjusted as best they could to a dynamic industrial sector. In Akron, for example, realtors reminded prospective buyers of "better properties" that their offerings were "west of the smoke." This real estate, located on the west side of the teeming Summit County seat, remained convenient to the centers of business and commerce, but prevailing winds helped to blow away the smoke of various rubber shops, factories, and railroad yards.

Capitalists and entrepreneurs liked Ohio, and they invested widely. The landscape was dotted with a plethora of industrial concerns: coal mines, oil and gas wells, brickyards, flour mills, and seemingly countless other businesses. A dramatic indication of the state's industrial might was the "flats" area along the Cuyahoga River in Cleveland, where a large and varied assortment of industrial concerns were situated, including metal foundries, oil refineries, and steel mills. But Cleveland was not the only place where smoke stack industries reigned; northeastern Ohio, most of all, emerged as one of America's great industrial centers. A contemporary resident rightly called the area the "Ruhr of America."

The Dexter City Roller Mill in Noble County seems to have passed its prime in this ca. 1910 picture postcard. *(Claibourne E. Griffin)*

Farmers living near the central Ohio hamlet of Basil could trade with D. S.
Cook & Company, a dealer in "Hay, Grain, Flour, Feed, and Seed," an
agribusiness facility that was common throughout the state.
(Claibourne E. Griffin)

Early on Ohioans began exploiting their abundant stands of timber. This Chesterland sawmill was likely constructed from the lumber it produced.
(Claibourne E. Griffin)

By the early years of the twentieth century, coal mining had grown into a major industry. Adena, Jefferson County, is in one of the prime coal-producing areas. This card shows Mine No. 1 of the Robey Coal Company. *(H. Roger Grant)*

OIL FIELD. — FLAGDALE — BREMEN O.

As the nineteenth century came to a close, widely scattered sections of the state enjoyed an oil and gas boom, as was the case with the "Flagdale" oil field near Bremen, Fairfield County. *(Claibourne E. Griffin)*

The electric light Plant is our town ... waite I felt good today ... delevery. as my old one are giving out then Hills are on an average three Hundred feet high. we are on the finish floor wouk. Best Love. & Regards

The Logan Brick Manufacturing Co., Logan, Ohio

Some of Ohio's abundant and commercially viable deposits of clay were good enough for the production of fine china ware, though most of these minerals were better suited for brick and tile products. The Logan Brick Manufacturing Company in Logan, Hocking County, is an example of the flourishing "mud" business. *(Claibourne E. Griffin)*

Rock deposits, suitable for construction purposes, developed into a significant business. In this view card, the camera captures a specially geared locomotive attached to a rock car at a quarry near Castalia in Erie County. *(H. Roger Grant)*

Railroads emerged as one of the first great employers in the state, and often the
initial wage-earning experience outside of agriculture for thousands of Ohio
youth involved a railroad job. The Erie Railroad shops in Kent, Portage County,
pumped large amounts of payroll and tax money into the local economy.
(H. Roger Grant)

252. SUPERIOR EXTENSION No. 1, ASHTABULA HARBOR, OHIO.

This postcard shows the harbor at Ashtabula alive with activity, with iron ore from the head of the lakes being moved by Hulett unloaders into railcars. Much of this tonnage would be destined for the steel mills of the Pittsburgh and Youngstown areas. George Hulett, inventor of this unloader, was a Clevelander who in 1890 began manufacturing coal- and ore-handling machinery.

(H. Roger Grant)

Carnegie Steel Co. (Ohio Steel Works and Furnaces)~Youngstown, Ohio.

The Carnegie Steel Company, which became the core of United States Steel
Corporation in 1901, operated the Ohio Steel Works in Youngstown.
(Claibourne E. Griffin)

In 1913 the card sender identifies this sprawling industrial facility as the "Mechanical Rubber Company" in Cleveland, adding, "Here's where I'm working now." *(H. Roger Grant)*

Where "Goodrich" Bands are Made

The B. F. Goodrich manufacturing complex on South Main Street in Akron helped make the "City at the Summit" the world's leading center of rubber production. *(Claibourne E. Griffin)*

The Taylor Chair Company in Bedford provided industrial jobs for residents of this thriving Cuyahoga County community. *(H. Roger Grant)*

The Dueber-Hampden Watch Works Canton, Ohio.

Canton boasted one of America's foremost watch makers, the Dueber-Hampden Watch Company. In 1888 local boosters lured the Dueber Watch Company of Newport, Kentucky, and the Hampden Watch Manufacturing Company from Springfield, Massachusetts, to the Stark County capital. *(H. Roger Grant)*

MT. VERNON BRIDGE WORKS, MT. VERNON, OHIO 21-13

Industrial firms employing large numbers of workers were scattered throughout Ohio. This real photo card of the Mt. Vernon Bridge Works plant site shows employees unloading steel from a gondola car. *(H. Roger Grant)*

The Dean Electric Company in Lorain made telephone equipment.
(H. Roger Grant)

Ohioans at Work

Because of a diverse economic base, Ohioans worked in a range of jobs. They mined coal, made steel, taught school, operated trains, sold merchandise, managed factories, tended farms, and raised families. Rates of employment for wage earners were generally high during the picture postcard era, even though a flood of immigration increased competition for unskilled and semi-skilled positions.

Ohio's industrial preeminence contributed to the building of trade unions. Coal miners, who tunneled into the bowels of the state, understandably grumbled about their working conditions and frequently low wages. In 1890 such concerns led to the formation of the United Mine Workers union in Columbus and the subsequent growth of the movement, with Ohio becoming a center of strength. A decade later national membership of the United Mine Workers of America stood at 55,000; 14,000 of these members lived in the Buckeye State. Thousands of other Ohioans banded together, and by the First World War nearly a score of unions maintained their national headquarters in the state, including the Brewery Workers, Brotherhood of Locomotive Engineers, and the International Molders Union.

Specific state statutes offered much as well. The revised Ohio Constitution of 1912 contained various pro-labor provisions, including mandatory workmen's compensation, "mechanic liens" on property to protect a laborer's equity, and the eight-hour day, "except in cases of extraordinary emergency." Thus, unionization and the rising tide of reform generally led to a better environment for Ohio workers.

A horse auction takes place near the entrance of the Harrison County jail in Cadiz. Horses commonly remained beasts of burden until after the First World War. *(Claibourne E. Griffin)*

A farm family in Fayette County, near Jeffersonville, stands near its poultry incubator. The Gem Incubator Company, located in Trotwood, boasted, "For strong, healthy chicks use GEM INCUBATORS AND BROODERS. They make good where others fail and the hen goes on laying the eggs." *(Claibourne E. Griffin)*

PICKERS WEIGHING IN THEIR BEANS
THE SCIOTO CANNING CO.
FACTORY AT ASHVILLE, O.

There was no generation gap when it came to farm work. Here bean pickers
(including children) for the Scioto Canning Company in Ashville, Pickaway
County, are in the process of weighing the fruits of their labors.
(Claibourne E. Griffin)

A gang of bridge laborers takes a break from working along the Cleveland, Akron & Columbus Railroad *(above)*, and the crew of a Detroit, Toledo & Ironton Railroad pile driver *(opposite)* poses for a photograph. *(H. Roger Grant)*

Although the Pennsylvania Railroad led the movement for employee pensions, it still found jobs for those who needed a paycheck, as with this "old flag man at Orrville," who drew a modest monthly income. *(H. Roger Grant)*

Draymen met the trains at the depot and transported freight, express, and mail. In this real photo card the drayman in West Mansfield has his wagon loaded with shipments of bread from the White Star Baking Company in Marysville and several sacks of U.S. mail. *(H. Roger Grant)*

Coal miners, probably in Stark County, pose for the camera before they enter the "pit." *(H. Roger Grant)*

These timber workers load a flatcar in Glenmont, Holmes County, ca. 1910.
(H. Roger Grant)

How do you like the ditch digger?

Following the devastating depression of the 1890s, Ohio municipalities invested heavily in their infrastructures. About 1914 water pipes were installed in West Salem, Wayne County. *(H. Roger Grant)*

With a plethora of wood frame structures, fire-fighting companies, whether professional or volunteer, were a necessity. Here a hook-and-ladder unit of the Lorain Fire Department stands in a city street. *(H. Roger Grant)*

This picture postcard describes what these Akron rubber workers are doing: *(top)* "The sheets of rubber in the drying room being inspected"; *(bottom)* "The sheets of smoked plantation crepe rubber being hung up to dry after it has been washed. It looks like a chamois hide."
(Claibourne E. Griffin)

HOW TIRES ARE MADE, AKRON, OHIO
DRYING THE CREPE RUBBER

PACKING DEPARTMENT OF THE M. HOMMEL WINE CO.,
SANDUSKY, OHIO.

The M. Hommel Wine Company of Sandusky distributed this card showing
workers in its packing department. *(Claibourne E. Griffin)*

Millinery shop employees of The Home Company in Ashland attend to the needs of their customers. *(H. Roger Grant)*

The owner of the Hub Dry Goods Store in Greenwich, in a prosperous agricultural section of Huron County, displays some of his shop's draperies and rugs. *(Claibourne E. Griffin)*

Residents are "dishing up for dinner" at the government-sponsored National Military Home near Dayton. *(Claibourne E. Griffin)*

GOV. HARMON AT TARGET PRACTICE. CAMP PERRY O.   .25·54

During a summer training session of the Ohio National Guard at Camp Perry in Ottawa County near Port Clinton, Governor Judson Harmon (1909–13) hones his shooting skills. *(Claibourne E. Griffin)*

A guard strolls down the long corridor of prison cells at the state reformatory in Mansfield. *(Claibourne E. Griffin)*

Ohioans at Play

In the early twentieth century Ohioans found leisure time to be at a premium. The modern weekend had yet to be "invented" and would not become common until after World War II. By the 1920s hope for more discretionary time increased, and those who labored in the construction and printing trades, for example, usually worked a five-day schedule. Ohioans, and their fellow Americans, who depended upon the wage system typically toiled at least fifty hours a week. Merchants commonly stayed open on Saturdays, including evenings until 8:00 or 9:00 P.M., to serve the "farm trade." Farmers themselves worked during much of the year; if they maintained herds of dairy cattle or other livestock, their winter months remained active with various chores.

Ohio's strong economic base and its nonpareil transportation network did much to provide residents with opportunities to enjoy their limited free time. Outings for individuals, families, and groups were popular by the turn of the century.

One historian equated the picnic with the trolley, and that relationship held true for the Buckeye State. Electric streetcars and interurbans conveniently and cheaply hauled Ohioans to amusement parks, dance halls, local spas, and picnic groves. Steam railroads, too, offered "specials" that took excursionists to ball games, circuses, and other attractions. And with the advent of motor cars and better roads, such destinations became more accessible.

Whatever the attraction or event, and whatever means to it, Ohioans bought picture postcards as souvenirs of the day.

Before the automobile became king, the "buggy ride" was an important pastime, especially on Sundays. This view shows three women who have stopped on a road in North Industry, Stark County. *(H. Roger Grant)*

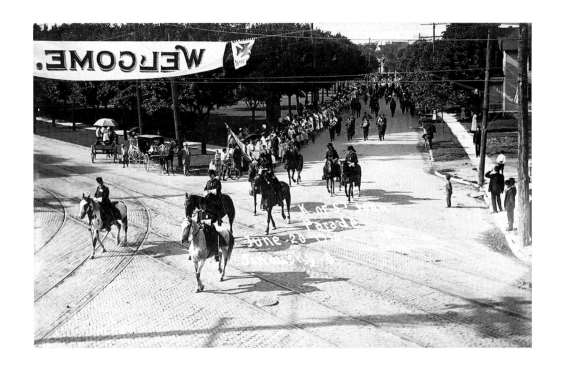

A Sandusky card-maker captured the excitement of a parade sponsored by the Knights of St. John, a fraternal organization. *(Claibourne E. Griffin)*

K. or St. John Sandusky O. June 20 1910

This senior class float added much to the annual Corn Festival parade, a popular summer event in Swanton, Fulton County. *(Claibourne E. Griffin)*

The "Royal Chariot" of the Wamba Carnival in Toledo attracts attention.
(Claibourne E. Griffin)

The Brighton Orchestra of Brighton in Lorain County is ready to play beautiful music. *(Claibourne E. Griffin)*

The Columbian Trio Concert Company of West Salem produced this advertising postcard. *(Claibourne E. Griffin)*

Columbian Trio Concert Co.

C.J.MYERS

A.C.FUHRMAN

B.F.WILLIAMS

SIXTEENTH SEASON

For Terms and Dates, Address West Salem, Ohio

"Smile and the world smiles with you;
Kick, and you go alone;
For a cheerful grin will let you in
Where a kicker is never known.

Hustle, a fortune awaits you;
Shirk, and defeat is sure.
For there's no chance for deliverance
To the chap who can't endure.

Kick, and there's trouble brewing;
Whistle, and life is gay;
This world's in tune like a day in June,
And the clouds all melt away."

OBERLIN COLLEGE GLEE CLUB, OBERLIN, OHIO.

These music makers form the Oberlin College Glee Club.
(Claibourne E. Griffin)

By the time of the First World War, Ohio's major cities were home to scores of such dance halls as Lorain's popular Palm Garden Pavilion. *(Claibourne E. Griffin)*

A party of bathers gathers on the shores of Lake Erie in Vermilion.
(Claibourne E. Griffin)

THE BATHING BEACH,   CEDAR POINT- ON LAKE ERIE.

The bathing beach at Cedar Point, near Sandusky, is somewhat less popular today than it was at the turn of the century. *(Claibourne E. Griffin)*

Tennis Court + Pump station Warner O

A mixed-doubles group plays tennis on a court in the village of Warner, Washington County, in ca. 1907. *(H. Roger Grant)*

Columbus Country Club

As with tennis, golf steadily attracted more participants, especially among the elite. The Columbus Country Club emerged as an important social center.
(H. Roger Grant)

VIEW OF SHADY SIDE PARK, CHAUTAUQUA AUDITORIUM, FREEPORT, OHIO.

Tent Chautauquas drew large numbers of Ohioans between about 1905 and 1925, with a number of communities even constructing special "Chautauqua Parks" for the traveling companies of actors, musicians, and speakers. Freeport, a village in Harrison County, has its Chautauqua Auditorium in Shady Side Park.

(Claibourne E. Griffin)

Ohioans and other Americans commonly feared the evil influences of the theater, which was gaining popularity among residents. *The Old Homestead,* by Denman Thompson attracted a faithful following during its run in Cleveland. As an advertisement read, "We were taken to see this charming play in our childhood days, because it was known and talked about in church and Sunday School circles as being one of the very few dramas that could be witnessed with perfect safety to the morals of the young." *(Claibourne E. Griffin)*

SEE MY NEW MITTENS. MOTHER KNIT THEM. I'M GOING TO HAVE CUFF BUTTONS WHEN I GROW UP.

FRANK THOMPSON Presents DENMAN THOMPSON'S
"THE OLD HOMESTEAD"
Hear the Famous Double Quartet   See the Beautiful Church Scene
Full Scenic Production   SEATS NOW ON SALE

PROSPECT Theatre, Cleveland
Week of OCTOBER 6
Matinees: Tuesday, Thursday and Saturday

BRING YOUR LITTLE MILKMAID WHEN THE COWS MARCH BY

B-8 TALBOTT-ENO CO., DES MOINES   MANSFIELD, OHIO, SEPT. 20-23, '10

County fairs and the circuses were popular attractions for Ohioans. The parade
of milk cows was a regular event at the Richland County Fair in Mansfield.
(Claibourne E. Griffin)

Carnival at Fairgrounds, Dayton, Ohio, given by The South Main Street Improvement Association, August 21-22-23, 1913

The carnival sponsored by the South Main Street Improvement Association in Dayton was well received *(above)*, and, similarly, residents of Shiloh in Richland County discovered that there was "something doing every minute" at their street fair and homecoming *(overleaf)*. *(Claibourne E. Griffin)*

MEET ME AT THE BIG

STREET FAIR AND

HOME COMING

Shiloh, O., Sept. 15 & 16, 1911

EVERYBODY ELSE WILL BE

THERE; WHY NOT YOU?

"SOMETHING DOING EVERY MINUTE"

WELCOME

JOYOUS BUCKEYE HOME COMING COLUMBUS SEPT. 2,3,4, 5,6. 1907

JOYOUS BUCKEYE HOME COMING COLUMBUS SEPT. 2,3,4, 5,6. 1907

Dear Boys! Will look for you tomorrow. Your Father

STREET SCENE IN OHIO'S CAPITAL.

Columbus hosted more than the Ohio State Fair. In 1907 the city welcomed the "Joyous Buckeye Home Coming." *(Claibourne E. Griffin)*

With kindest Greeting of the season

THE OAK

AN IDEAL PLACE FOR REST AND COMFORT. *Laura Batschu* HARRISON, OHIO.

Some Ohioans spent leisure time in inns, like ones in Harrison, Hamilton County *(above)*; Seaman, Adams County *(opposite)*; and Willoughby, Lake County *(overleaf)*. *(Claibourne E. Griffin & H. Roger Grant)*

GOOD AS ANY, BETTER'N SOME.

THIS IS THE SPARGUR HOUSE,

FRANK G. YOUNG, Prop., SEAMAN, O.

Special attractions caught the fancy of Ohioans, including this "air ship" in Toledo. *(H. Roger Grant)*

The Fresh Air Farm in Terrace Park near Cincinnati offers disadvantaged youth the brief opportunity to escape the urban environment. *(Claibourne E. Griffin)*

At the Fresh Air Farm   Terrace Park O.

A Group of Boys, Cleveland Boys' Home, Hudson, Ohio

A group of youngsters from the Cleveland Boys' Home near Hudson is apparently on an expedition. *(Claibourne E. Griffin)*

In 1907 members of a YMCA organization in Canton break from their camp activities. *(H. Roger Grant)*

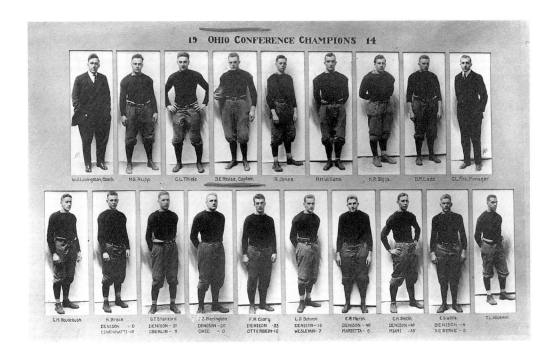

Football games developed enthusiastic followings. In 1914 the Denison
University team, which won the Ohio Conference Championship that year, is
the subject of a special picture postcard. *(H. Roger Grant)*

Street and interurban railways usually operated at least one amusement park, such as Lake Hiawatha Park in Mt. Vernon, the self-proclaimed "Ohio's Beauty Spot," which could be reached by a local trolley. *(H. Roger Grant)*

(Above and overleaf) Silver Lake, promoted by the Northern Ohio Traction &
Light Company, attracted thousands of northeastern Ohio residents each year,
many from nearby Akron. *(Claibourne E. Griffin & H. Roger Grant)*

The Pavilion, Silver Lake, near Akron, O. 4/17/04

I will soon be corresponding with the entire family. W X, O,

When Ohioans visited amusement parks or resorts, they had opportunities to have made commemorative picture postcards of themselves. A baby is shown at Buckeye Lake east of Columbus in Licking County *(right)*, and a group of women is photographed at Myers Lake near Canton *(overleaf)*. *(Claibourne E. Griffin)*

While a product of a local studio and not from a photo gallery at an amusement park, this picture postcard of an Akron family shows them dreaming about the wonders of air travel. *(Claibourne E. Griffin)*

Ohio in Historic Postcards
was composed in 11/16 Adobe Caslon
on a Gateway 486 PC using Adobe PageMaker
at The Kent State University Press;
printed by offset lithography
on 70-pound Luna Matte stock
(an acid-free paper),
notch case bound over 98' binder's boards
in Arrestox B cloth on the spine
with side panels of 80-pound Rainbow Oatmeal A stock,
endpapers of Rainbow Ivory A stock,
and wrapped with dust jackets printed in four color process
on 100-pound enamel stock
finished with matte film lamination
by Friesens Printers, Canada;
designed and composed by Will Underwood;
and published by
The Kent State University Press
KENT, OHIO 44242 USA